DEDICATION

To everyone who makes Reno, *RENO*.
Your passion for this community has
made it what it is today—a fascinating,
welcoming, spectacular place to call home.
Thank you for creating a loving place for
the most important people in my world.

CONTENTS

• •

100

THINGS TO DO IN

RENO

BEFORE YOU

DIE

2nd Edition

Sparks Marina

100 THINGS TO DO IN RENO BEFORE YOU DIE

2nd Edition

MIKALEE BYERMAN

Reedy Press
PO Box 5131
St. Louis, MO 63139, USA
www.reedypress.com

Library of Congress Control Number: 2023938693

ISBN: 9781681064697

Design by Jill Halpin

Special thanks to visitrenotahoe.com for most of the editorial photos, including the cover image, and to Sally Casas with Modern Muse Photography for the author photo.

Printed in the United States of America
23 24 25 26 27   5 4 3 2 1

Music and Entertainment

Sports and Recreation

Culture and History

Shopping and Fashion

ACKNOWLEDGMENTS

Seven years ago, I used this space to thank my kids—then two teens and a toddler.

Now I have two adults and a tween. Time is weird.

But despite the weirdness of time, I'm so blessed to watch them all do life. And by the way, having adult kids is super cool—solid five stars.

So to Dylan: Thank you for always making me laugh. Your constant quirkiness brings joy to my life, and I'm so proud of your choices and career. To Megan: Thank you for loving my son . . . and for being a beautiful addition to our family.

To Jilleann: Thank you for all the talks. Every single one of them. I'm so grateful for your perspective, strength, and spirit; watching from the sidelines as you "adult" fills me with unspeakable delight.

To Bryerlee: Thank you for loving simple dinners (usually involving cheese) so that I could focus on writing. And I love how we begin each day documenting three things we're grateful for—please know that you, your brother, and your sister are forever at the tippy-top of my list.

To my parents, Sharon and Jim: Please know how indescribably grateful I am for you. Your generosity—with time and care for my family (and sweet puppy!)—never goes unnoticed.

Now to a partial list of people who've been connection points and inspo for locations in the book: Rachel Gattuso, Nettie Oliverio, Sally Casas, Sharon and Steven Ing, Lynnette Bellin, Megg Mueller, Steve Zuchowski, Courtney Meredith, Dave Archer, Ben McDonald, Jackie Shelton, Kathy Powers, Katie Coombs, Chris Tisdale, Terri Ogden, Tracie Barnthouse, Kevin Ciccotti, Devon Reese, Dave Santina, Geralda Miller, Brooke Santina, South Reno Moms Facebook group, and Team Travel Nevada.

And to Heidi and Phil Currey: Thank you for accompanying me on adventures—and for not giving creepy junkyard dude my phone number.

PREFACE

As you've likely noticed, this is the second edition of *100 Things to Do in Reno Before You Die*, and I joked in the first edition's preface that writing it was like the *Sophie's Choice* of books. Which places should I feature? Which places do I skip? How will that make the skipped spots feel? (Clearly I'm an empath, and yes, my therapist has warned me that it's unhealthy to ascribe feelings to inanimate objects.)

But quite obviously, the Reno landscape has changed considerably since 2017, meaning this second edition inspired me to go through a whole new round of Sophie's choice. When I was trying to narrow down one particularly tough category, it was my dear friend Sharon Ing who reminded me, "But is that a place to go *before you die*?"

All of this is to say: this is not intended to be a comprehensive guide to all the places that make Northern Nevada spectacular. That would take multiple editions of countless volumes. This is simply 100 experiences as curated by me, a middle-aged single mom, a writer, a lover of Reno, a two-time University of Nevada graduate, a former chief marketing officer of Nevada's tourism division, a woman who distrusts tomatoes because of their creepy texture.

I wrote this book as a reflection of my passion for this community—with abundant help from tomato-loving friends who could offer their alternate perspective on Reno experiences as well.

• •

So please, join me at “100 Things to Do in Reno Before You Die” on Facebook, find me on LinkedIn, or connect with me via my website at MikaleeByerman.com. Tell me what you love about this book, and tell me what I missed. We can also commiserate about how that location must feel—considering I so dismissively ignored it.

It’ll be like therapy, but cheaper.

Hub Coffee Roasters

FOOD AND DRINK

1

GET A TASTE OF HISTORY
AT CASALE'S HALFWAY CLUB

Looking for the chance to pay homage to the origins of Reno's food scene? These two restaurants are oldies but goodies.

If there is an iconic, truly Reno experience, you'll find it at Casale's Halfway Club, which opened its doors in 1937. As unpretentious as it is rich in history, you'll want to spend time soaking up homestyle history with the Casale clan, who still serve their traditional, handmade, family recipes direct from Italy.

Don't be surprised by the cold red wine (it's a family favorite), but do expect to leave feeling like you just experienced the finest lasagna, ravioli, and spaghetti you'll ever taste.

Or visit "The Coney," which started as a tamale factory in the 1920s but evolved into its current iteration in 1945—and is now operated by the third generation of the Galletti family. Heritage is evident throughout this Sparks landmark, which is open six days a week for lunch (Galletti's Spaghetti is a Tuesday favorite), and for two Friday dinner seatings.

Casale's Halfway Club
2501 E 4th St., 775-323-3979 (reservations recommended)
casaleshalfwayclub.com

Coney Island
2644 Prater Way, Sparks, 775-358-6485
coneyislandbar.net

2

STEAK YOUR CLAIM
AT CHURRASCO BRAZILIAN STEAKHOUSE

If you're feeling particularly carnivorous, Northern Nevada has many rare options that'll leave you exclaiming "Well done!"

First up, Churrasco Brazilian Steakhouse serves 15 all-you-can-eat rotisserie-grilled meats in traditional rodízio fashion: gauchos—Brazilian cowboys—approach the table with grilled meats on a giant metal skewer, they slice them with an impressive knife, and you use your adorable mini tongs to add them to your plate. Then there's the buffet-style fresh market table, featuring 50 hot sides and chilled salads (don't skip the mushroom risotto!).

Or for a more traditional take on a steakhouse, an unexpected gem known as Western Village Steakhouse can be found inside a popular local casino. The surprisingly affordable destination offers tableside salad preparation, indulgent appetizers, and steaks that melt in your mouth. But you MUST save room for dessert, and request the tableside preparation of bananas foster, cherries jubilee, or coffee diablo (each prepared for two or more).

Churrasco Brazilian Steakhouse
425 S Virginia St., 775-322-4000
churrascobr.com

Western Village Steakhouse
815 Nichols Blvd., Sparks, 775-353-4916
westernvillagesparks.com

3

FIND YOUR COMFORT (FOOD) ZONE
AT BRASSERIE ST. JAMES

In the mood for something completely indulgent?

Brasserie St. James is housed in the historic Crystal Springs building in Midtown, which translates to a rustic decor (complete with a deer mount and a fireplace that roars during cooler months). Unique pub food is the core of this charming restaurant, but the real scene-stealing dish is the mac 'n' cheese: served bubbly hot, bathing in creamy gruyere and sharp cheddar. They'll add cauliflower, mushrooms, and leeks for a slight upcharge—and it's totally worth it. For another indulgent offering, try Basque mussels with chorizo, fennel, tomatoes, garlic, and white wine.

But if soup is more the mood of the day, there's one place to cure that warm-and-cozy craving: Süp, of course. Born from the owners' tradition of "Soup Sunday" get-togethers for friends and family at their home, they've been serving healthy homemade recipes made from scratch since 2007. Check their menu for daily options (many gluten-free), and try their mouthwatering salads and sandwiches.

Brasserie St. James
901 S Center St., 775-348-8888
brasseriesaintjames.com

Süp
669 S Virginia St., 775-324-4787
sup.restaurant

4

BREAK YOUR FAST
AT HOMEGROWN GASTROPUB

Rise and shine at these two breakfast favorites—they'll make it worth your while to be a Northern Nevada early bird.

Organic food fresh from local farms is the forte at Homegrown Gastropub, and while they're open daily until midnight for all dining options, breakfast is a must. Favorites include the vegetarian brick-oven frittata (the basement houses a wood-fired oven) made with organic eggs, fresh herbs, seasonal veggies, natural goat cheese, and house chipotle crema. Or go decadent and order the apple cinnamon deep-dish French toast, topped with caramelized apples and freshly whipped cream.

Or stop by one of Two Chicks's two locations—after visiting their website to appreciate the many sweary chicken puns. From skillets to omelets to benedicts to the best clucking grilled cheese sandwiches you'll ever have (inspired by their sister location, GourMelt, in Sparks), you're sure to find an "egg-celent" new breakfast favorite.

Homegrown Gastropub
719 S Virginia St., 775-683-9989
homegrowngastropub.com

Two Chicks
752 S Virginia St.
5851 S Virginia St.
775-323-0600
twochicksreno.com

5

LAND A (PICON) PUNCH
AT LOUIS' BASQUE CORNER

Northern Nevada is renowned for its Basque heritage, as waves of immigrants in the American West turned to sheepherding in the rugged mountains when the California Gold Rush ran dry. So it makes sense that one local beverage pays culinary homage to this rich history.

And while soups, garlicky meat, and abundant fries are always on the informal, family-friendly table at Louis' Basque Corner, the before-and-after-dinner highlight is from the bar: Nevada's unofficial state drink, the Picon punch.

Recipes vary depending on the part of Nevada (and the particular bar) you're in, but a traditional Picon has grenadine, a float of brandy, a lemon peel, and Amer Picon, a hard-to-find bittersweet French liqueur with a unique nutty orange flavor.

A word of warning: stop at two. As Louis' Basque's namesake and former owner—Louis Erreguible—is known for saying: "The first two are the Picon, the third is the punch."

Louis' Basque Corner
301 E 4th St., 775-323-7203
louisbasquecorner.com

6

DISCOVER A WHOLE NEW WORLD AT ALADDIN'S MARKET & KITCHEN

Looking for the fresh flavors of the Mediterranean while in Northern Nevada? Unexpectedly, you can find them in all their authentic glory at Aladdin's. The "Market" part means you can shop here for ingredients to cook yourself; the "Kitchen" is where the owner's family saves you the work!

Walking into Aladdin's, you'll likely be greeted by Radi Rejoub, who opened Midtown's first Mediterranean market in 2014. Engage him in conversation, and you'll learn he came to Reno from Jordan to study civil engineering at the University of Nevada, Reno. After the 2008 Recession, he pivoted careers (he was building custom homes) to instead build a family business.

Browse the market's considerable selection of spices and seasonings, pastas and legumes, teas, and infused waters. Then, order a selection from the digital board boasting 100 percent halal-certified, wholesome food. You can't go wrong with the falafel sandwich—bathed lightly in tahini and garlic sauce and adorned with lettuce, pickles, cucumbers, red onions, and tomatoes. It's like something magical delivered by a genie from a lamp.

1180 Holcomb Ave., 775-737-4244
aladdinsmarketreno.com

7

EAT, DRINK, AND GOSSIP
AT YELP TOP 100'S RICE BOX KITCHEN

Fun fact: Reno has not only one, but THREE Yelp Top 100 restaurants. And astoundingly, one of them is the delectable creation of a self-taught cook who holds an interior design/art degree. Perapol, chef/owner of Rice Box Kitchen, learned to cook authentic Thai dishes from his mother, eventually opening the "underground" Gossip Kitchen in San Francisco. But Reno is now blessed with its own very above-ground, delicious experience. Try the simple but sublime Khao Mun Gai, a traditional Thai street food of poached skinless chicken thigh over coconut-ginger rice. Or come for a Sunday high-tea dim sum seating or an all-you-can-eat, Thai-style shabu-shabu dinner.

But don't stop there, as you'll want to try the other two Yelp Top 100s too: Arario and La Condesa. At Arario, you'll be inspired by the Korean-fusion menu featuring small plates and favorites such as the bulgogi bowl and bibimbap. And La Condesa is a different kind of fusion—Spanish and Mexican, Asian and Italian, traditional and contemporary—all in a modern setting.

TIP

Yelp Top 100 restaurants are chosen from a pool of nationwide nominees. Visit Yelp Reno's robust community page to learn more about these foodie hot spots. You'll find pictures and person-on-the-street reviews to help you choose your next date-night destination.

instagram.com/yelpreno

Rice Box Kitchen
555 S Virginia St., Ste. 103, 775-384-3401
riceboxkitchen.com

Arario Midtown
777 S Center St., Ste. 200, 775-870-8202
arariomidtown.com

La Condesa Eatery
1642 S Wells Ave., 775-409-3000
lacondesaeatery.com

8

JUMP IN THE LINE
AT FOOD TRUCK FRIDAY

Reno has an ever-evolving food truck scene, but keep in mind the allure of food truck culture: it often involves standing in lines, but it typically serves up incredible food. Avoid the need to ride around town in search of your dinner by visiting one of Reno's two best food truck experiences: Food Truck Friday, produced by Reno Street Food, and Feed the Camel.

Food Truck Friday brings about 45 food, dessert, and drink vendors to Idlewild Park every Friday night in summer. It's one of the nation's top five largest weekly food truck events.

Feed the Camel happens seasonally on Wednesday nights (hump day, thus the "camel" reference) under the Keystone Bridge at the McKinley Arts and Culture Center. This is a food truck event combined with an arts bazaar.

Food Truck Friday
Idlewild Park, 2055 Idlewild Dr., 775-825-2665
renofoodtruckfriday.com

Feed the Camel
McKinley Arts and Culture Center, 925 Riverside Dr.
facebook.com/feedthecamel
instagram.com/feedthecamel

SAVOR THE OLD-SCHOOL ATMOSPHERE AT JOHNNY'S

If Italian food is the way to your heart, Northern Nevada has a menu of choices for you to consider. Here are two special options.

A favorite for generations of Renoites celebrating special occasions, Johnny's Ristorante Italiano is old-school Reno meets classic Italian specialties of the carne, pasta, and pesce variety. Don't skip one of their signature dishes: a filet of petrale sole in a delightful lemon sauce. Go for the fabulous food, but drink in the atmosphere and relish the attentive service reminiscent of days gone by.

A strip mall in Reno is hardly the place you'd expect to run taste-first into Old World Italy, but that's exactly what you'll find at Zozo's Ristorante. The exposed brick-lined walls, red-and-white checkered tablecloths, and grapevine-and-latticework ceiling provide the dazzling backdrop to a delectable culinary experience. Enjoy fishbowl-sized glasses of wine, baskets of mouthwatering garlic bread, and the best seafood cioppino in town.

Johnny's Ristorante Italiano
4245 W 4th St., 775-747-4511
johnnysristorante.com

Zozo's Ristorante
3446 Lakeside Dr., 775-829-9449
zozosreno.com

10

WINE DOWN
AT WHISPERING VINE

Craving a glass of wine that won't break the bank? Here are three places to try before you die (of thirst).

Whispering Vine's largest location is in a historic 4th Street building that longtime Renoites still call The Glory Hole—which we swear, was a steakhouse named for a once-popular mining term. Here, they feature a delightful menu that you can enjoy in different enclaves of the building, each with its own personality. Eat, drink, and then shop for a bottle (or several, no judgment here) for later. With two locations in town, you'll find a Whispering Vine that speaks to your wine-loving heart.

But perhaps you're in Sparks. Never fear, because Engine 8 Urban Winery—a winery-plus-fancy-snacks destination owned by native Nevadans—is at your service. Enjoy live music on some weekend evenings in a casual, cozy atmosphere.

Speaking of atmosphere, Blackrock Wine Co. has arguably the largest outdoor patio for wine-ing and dining in southwest Reno—plus an ever-changing global wine and craft beer selection and creative small plates.

Whispering Vine Wine Co.
Multiple locations, 775-786-1323
whisperingvinewine.com

Engine 8 Urban Winery
1260 Avenue of the Oaks, Ste. 150, Sparks, 775-996-3648
engine8urbanwinery.com

Blackrock Wine Co.
6135 Lakeside Dr., Ste. 111, 775-440-1091
blackrockwineco.com

11

TAKE A TASTY TOUR OF ASIA

STARTING AT KAUBOI IZAKAYA

Asian influences are making their mark on Reno's restaurant scene. So pull out your map, and let's globe-trot without leaving Reno!

First stop: Japan. Kauboi (pronounced "kuh'-boy") means "cowboy," and Izakaya translates roughly to "stay saké shop," so Kauboi Izakaya is a rustic cowboy-themed bar/restaurant where you'll enjoy a tapas-style Japanese experience. Sit at the bar opposite the grill for dinner and a show. It can be loud, so be prepared to lip-read if you're on a date. And no reservations here—come early or late!

Our next destination is China (ish)—with a visit to Kwok's Asian Bistro. The "ish" is because this is billed as Chinese-Asian fusion, with specialties that focus on freshness—that's the domain of the chef's nightly dinner specials. On the menu, you'll find favorites such as traditional claypots, duck, and delightful pork belly sliders.

We end in Thailand, with a visit to Moo Dang. Here, traditional Thai classics meet fun modern influences. You'll find spicy Thai soups, traditional pad Thai, curry, drunken noodles, and more.

Kauboi Izakaya
1286 S Virginia St., 775-453-2592

Kwok's Asian Bistro
275 West St., 775-507-7270
kwoksbistro.com

Moo Dang
1565 S Virginia St., 775-420-4267
thaimoodang.com

HONE YOUR "CRAFT"
AT GREAT BASIN BREWERY

If you're going to take a tour of Northern Nevada's expansive craft brewery and distillery scene, the first stop has to be the classic Great Basin Brewery, which bills itself as Nevada's oldest currently operating brewery. In fact, the brewery got its start the very year Nevada's state legislature legalized brewpubs—1993 (interesting, considering all the nefarious "practices" that were legal in Nevada decades before).

And at Great Basin, start with an Icky—named after Nevada's state fossil, the ichthyosaur.

The independent craft and distillery scene in Reno is thriving. Although there are too many destinations to mention them all, your best bet after visiting Great Basin is to make a personalized version of the Reno brewery map you'll find at visitrenotahoe.com/brewery-map. (Tip: you can even search for dog-friendly bars!)

You can also stop by The Eddy, a seasonal beer garden on the Riverwalk, to sample several close-by favorites.

Multiple locations
greatbasinbrewingco.com

SEEKING ETERNAL HOPPY-NESS? HERE ARE A FEW MORE FAVORITES TO WHET YOUR APPETITE

The Depot Craft Brewery & Distillery
325 E 4th St., 775-737-4330
thedepotreno.com

Pigeon Head
840 E 5th St., 775-276-6766
pigeonheadbrewery.com

IMBĪB Custom Brews
785 E 2nd St., 775-470-5996
imbibreno.com

Black Rabbit Mead Company
401 E 4th St., 775-410-6198
blackrabbitmeads.com

Schussboom Brewing
12245 S Virginia St., 775-900-3930
schussboombrewing.com

10 Torr Distilling and Brewing
490 Mill St., 775-499-5276
10torr.com

The Brewer's Cabinet
475 S Arlington Ave., 775-348-7481
thebrewerscabinet.com

Beer NV Taproom & Spirits
15 Foothill Rd., Ste. 1, 775-448-6199
beernv.com

Lead Dog Brewing
Reno and Sparks locations, 775-391-5110
leaddogbrewing.com

13

DIG UP CULINARY TREASURES
AT THE NUGGET CASINO RESORT

The Nugget Casino Resort in Sparks is an iconic part of local history. And while it makes its literal mark on the landscape as the tallest spot in Sparks, it's also an enduring contributor to the region's culinary scene.

A welcoming aroma of richly flavored seafood wafts over you as you enter the Oyster Bar thanks to a series of specialty steam pots atop the centerpiece bar, percolating the restaurant's signature dish. It's all about the velvety pan roast at the Oyster Bar, handmade with cream, butter, and decadent seafood.

Another specialty at the Nugget: surprisingly elevated upscale dining at Anthony's Chophouse. If you're lucky, you'll visit during one of their winemaker dinners, featuring exceptional food and wine pairings. Anthony's offers more than 350 wines (some encased in a glass wine case, which serves as a focal point separating the bar and dining room). Given the expansive selection, it's no surprise that the restaurant's general manager, Art, is a master sommelier—and loves to offer insight into the many varieties.

1100 Nugget Ave., Sparks
775-356-3300, x3772 (Oyster Bar) or x3801 (Anthony's Chophouse)
nuggetcasinoresort.com

SAY *¡SALUD!* WITH A MARGARITA AT LOS COMPADRES

Maybe the best aspect of a margarita is its omni-seasonality; whether it's 100 degrees outside or a blizzard, the flavorful drink is the perfect complement to authentic Mexican food. And perhaps the best margarita in town is served at Los Compadres, founded in 1995 by Rafael Valencia and his family. Rafael wanted to create the American dream, and, in doing so, he established a restaurant with a perfectly dreamy happy hour.

Dine on the patio between 4 and 6 p.m. weekdays for drink specials and appetizers. Or belly up to the bar on any evening after the dinner rush, and you might see a crew of regulars playing dice and imbibing. The aforementioned house-made margaritas blend a margarita mix that's made fresh daily with a generous helping of tequila. *¡Perfecto!*

Tomás is one of the joint's best bartenders. Begin a conversation with him, and he might jokingly say, "You can call me 'Honey' after your second margarita." Perhaps needless to say, Honey makes exceptional margaritas.

1250 Disc Dr., Sparks, 775-800-1822
25 Foothill Rd., 775-284-1301
loscompadresreno.com

15

STROLL, SIP, SNACK, AND DINE
ON RENO'S RIVERSIDE DRIVE

Local businesses are thriving along scenic Riverside Drive in Reno, which includes seven beautiful business and residential blocks that overlook the gurgling (or raging, depending on the season) Truckee River.

You'll first want to walk, bike, or drive to Hub Coffee Roasters, which has an expansive patio from which you'll watch the river while sipping your favorite caffeinated concoction. Then, hop next door to Dorinda's Chocolates, picking out a confection or two for your afternoon of relaxation along the Truckee corridor.

Finally, perhaps at the end of a day hiking, biking, or enjoying a book on a blanket alongside the banks of the Truckee River, freshen up and then return to the glorious Riverside Drive scene for a fine-dining experience at Beaujolais Bistro. Owner and chef Bill Gilbert offers a seasonally changing, modern-inspired French menu nightly. Enjoy cocktails at the charming bar, and then prepare yourself for one of Reno's finest dining experiences.

Hub Coffee Roasters
727 Riverside Dr., 775-453-1911
hubcoffeeroasters.com

Dorinda's Chocolates
727 Riverside Dr., Ste. E, 775-451-5972
dorindaschocolates.com

Beaujolais Bistro
753 Riverside Dr., 775-323-2227
beaujolaisbistro.com

16

RAISE A GLASS
TO THE RIVERWALK WINE WALK

You may know Reno as the "Biggest Little City in the World," but here's another take: with more than 70 bars, restaurants, and nightclubs within walking distance around the Reno arch, we're also the self-proclaimed (but as yet undisputed) Crawl Capital of the World.

You'll regularly bump into groups of Santas, leprechauns, or zombies while wandering downtown Reno during a crawl—all depending on the season. So, buy a glass, get a map, don your wristband, and explore the local bar scene—while dressed in your finest onesie.

And it's common knowledge that once you crawl, you walk: visit Reno on any third Saturday of the month, and you'll experience the Riverwalk District Wine Walk.

If the above doesn't sound like your cup of tea (or wine/beer), how about drinking while pedaling? Reno Brew Bike offers you the chance to roll around town, all while getting your drink (and exercise) on.

Crawl Reno
775-624-8320
crawlreno.com

Reno Brew Bike
775-771-0164
renobrewbike.com

Reno Riverwalk District Wine Walk
775-825-WALK (9255)
renoriver.org/wine-walk

17

WATCH THE TRANQUIL TRUCKEE

AT WILD RIVER GRILLE

In Reno, a river runs through it—downtown, that is—creating abundant options for scenic dining (with your furry friends) while overlooking the glorious Truckee River.

In the base of the historic Riverside, Wild River Grille has an expansive patio with heat lamps for cooler Reno evenings. Enjoy live music during warmer months as the sun sets behind the Riverwalk. Happy hour (with some of the best hummus in town) is a must. Or if you're Broadway-bound at the Pioneer Center, visit for dinner or dessert.

Just a bit upstream, longtime Reno restauranteurs MaryBeth and Chef Colin Smith established an American bistro called Smith and River. Upscale and modern, cozy and comfortable, they offer creative takes on traditional entrees—and a cocktail menu with signature drinks like the aptly named Mr. and Mrs. Smith.

Or visit The Shore just inside the Renaissance Reno Downtown Hotel, where they offer an exceptional weekday happy hour or a weekend brunch—inside or riverside.

Wild River Grille
17 S Virginia St., 775-284-7455
wildrivergrille.com

The Shore
1 S Lake St., 775-321-5831
shoreroom.com

Smith and River
50 N Sierra St., Ste. 104, 775-357-8019
smithandriver.com

18

MIMIC MIYAGI'S CHOPSTICK SKILLS
AT TOKYO SUSHI

Will you be catching flies with those bad boys? Not even. Instead, you'll be enjoying an experience that Reno has made famous: AYCE sushi (yup, ALL you can eat) for lunch or dinner at most local establishments, including local fave Tokyo Sushi.

Pull a barstool up to the sushi bar at Tokyo Sushi, strike up a conversation with the chefs, and they'll likely help you out by offering guidance about their own favorites. Most AYCE lunch/dinner locations include unlimited appetizers (shout-out to those fabulous mussels!), long- or hand-rolls with cooked or uncooked options, nigiri, and one dessert per paying customer.

Resistance to the Reno sushi trend is futile; bring your appetite and your mad chopstick skills, and be prepared for anything—and a little bit of everything. Because sushi is so popular locally, expect to wait. But it's worth it!

Tokyo Sushi
1999 S Virginia St.
775-825-8828
tokyosushireno.com

Hiroba Sushi
1495 E Prater Way, Ste. 113, Sparks
775-470-8177
hirobasushinv.com

Sushimi's
3005 Skyline Blvd., Ste. 160
775-829-2788
sushimisreno.com

Kei Sushi
5085 S McCarran Blvd.
775-657-9257
keisushi.com

SPOTLIGHT

Ready to travel outside of your sushi comfort zone? Visit Hinoki O, where the "O" stands for "omakase"—which translates to "I leave it up to you."

The concept: A sophisticated sushi diner knows to allow the menu to be guided by the sushi chef, thus at Hinoki O, the choice is out of your hands. So this interactive and intimate experience is curated entirely by the tastes of the chef and the ingredients at hand.

Expect a chef's choice sampling, all fish on rice, with a fixed price. And note there are only two seatings a night, with only four to six people per seating—with reservations required, usually many weeks out.

Hinoki O
7500 Rancharrah Pkwy., Ste. 110
facebook.com/hinokiomakase

TAP INTO TAPAS
AT CENTRO

Small plates are having a big moment, and quite a few Reno restaurants are in on the trend.

Visit the Midtown Centro location (pronounced the Italian way, so it's "chentro") for a metropolitan tour of tasty tapas. Centro is an ideal date destination, and sampling each other's filthy fries or sticky ribs will provide the perfect foundation for endless flirtation. Chef/owner Alberto Gazzola entices diners with dishes that pay homage to his northern Italian heritage, folding in influences from other international locales such as Asia and South America.

Close by, Midtown Spirits Wine & Bites also has an extensive selection of small bites. Bring your friends to sample snacks and more than 80 wines—plus frequent live entertainment, including Jazz Sundays.

Plus, there's Twisted Fork—its quirky name providing a glimpse into the Alice-through-the-looking-glass world of Latin-influenced, uber-creative dishes. While it has an expansive menu, introduce yourself by way of its seasonal, scrumptious small plates such as the tamal, ceviche, and pastor pork tacos.

Centro
236 California Ave., 775-737-9062
centroreno.com

Midtown Spirits Wine & Bites
1527 S Virginia St., 775-384-6002
midtownspiritswine.com

Twisted Fork
1191 Steamboat Pkwy., Ste. 1400, 775-853-6033
twistedforkreno.com

20

SAY "CHEESE" (AND MORE)
AT VINO'S PIZZA

If you're crazy about the 'za, has Reno got options! Check out these locations offering melty, cheesy, gooey goodness—and well, well beyond!

Stop by Vino's Pizza, with two Northern Nevada locations (and rumors of another location, coming soon!). If you're a shrimp fan, the Finding Nemo pizza is unparalleled. The thin-crust Cefalu is atypical—don't expect rich red sauce, but instead enjoy a nutty pesto—and it's super flavorful. Owner Vino cooks everything by hand, including sauces and dressings. If you visit on Wednesdays, wine is 50 percent off! Yes: Vino the owner has a nice selection of vino . . . because we like symmetry.

Another favorite is South Creek Pizza, where pizzas bake in about 90 seconds flat thanks to a 900-degree wood-fired brick oven imported from Naples, mozzarella is made fresh daily, and artisan Neapolitan-style dough is imported from Italy. Experience these quality touches while enjoying small plates or a handcrafted pizza.

Vino's Pizza
2888 Vista Blvd., Sparks, 775-622-3220
3228 N Carson St., Carson City, 775-887-7437
vinospizzanv.com

South Creek Pizza Co.
45 Foothill Rd., 775-622-1620
southcreekpizza.com

TIP

You can't control the timing of cravings for all things pizza parlor, so head to Noble Pie for a weekend brunch that—let's face it—might just inspire a carb coma. Yes, you'll find options such as a brunch slice, which is an uncommon take on pizza made with prosciutto and veggies, topped with a fry-poached egg and spicy hollandaise. But you'll also meet the best fried pizza dough ever in the form of their "sweet-cinn ricotta knots" and the "Badasserole"—made with challah, breakfast sausage, and parmesan garlic fries; baked with eggs and cream; and topped with green chile crema.

Midtown: 777 S Center St., 775-323-1494
Summit: 13979 S Virginia, Ste. 505, 775-298-1261
noblepieparlor.com

21

SATISFY YOUR SWEET TOOTH
AT PERENN BAKERY

Craving something sweet? Reno's got you covered. Locally owned and operated, these favorites will keep you coming back for more.

What started as a quaint bakery called Perenn in Midtown is now a legacy of deliciousness—in addition to their two Reno locations, they recently opened a "Greek-ish" rotisserie restaurant called Claio. The husband-wife owners met studying at the Culinary Institute of America and now offer their carefully crafted baked goods, plus sandwiches, salads, and more. The hands-down local favorite is the to-die-for handmade croissants.

But if donuts are more your speed, opt for the fresh, fluffy, and fabulous offerings at DoughBoys Donuts. Show your UNR pride by picking a Wolf Pack Paw, a raised donut shaped like a wolf paw, or grab the Big Boy, an 8-inch-diameter giant donut that serves 12. Owner Jay Kenny fulfills his #DoughGood mission through community support, making this sweet treat extra special.

Perenn
20 St. Lawrence Ave., Midtown
7700 Rancharrah Pkwy., Ste. 110
775-842-1508
perennbakery.com

DoughBoys Donuts
Locations in northwest Reno, south Reno, and Spanish Springs/Sparks
doughboysreno.com

PRIX FIXE YOUR SIGHTS
ON FOURK KITCHEN RENO

Do you read the last page of a book so you have a sense of how it all ends? If so, prix fixe dining—where the menu is predetermined, as is the cost—may be perfect for you!

Our first stop is Fourk Kitchen Reno for formal four-course dining that is casual and interactive. It's also reasonably priced, with a set per-person cost that's far more affordable than typical fine dining. The night starts with happy hour, followed by a welcome from the chef with an overview of what to expect. With one seating nightly and a different four-course meal every month, you'll want to make reservations again and again.

Another destination frequently offering incredibly special prix fixe dinners—either in celebration of a holiday or in collaboration with a local business—is Calafuria, though they're also open most weekend evenings with a more traditional dinner menu. Check their website or social media for upcoming options.

Fourk Kitchen Reno
4991 S Virginia St., Ste. B, 775-870-1000
fourkkitchen.com

Calafuria
725 S Center St., 775-360-5175
calafuriareno.com

23

DRINK IN THE ATMOSPHERE
AT RUM SUGAR LIME

Travel through time and place with a cocktail in hand while visiting these three iconic Reno bars:

If "Tiki Chic" were a style, its flagship location would be Rum Sugar Lime. But don't imagine kitschy tropical themes from the past—instead, envision a menu with elevated rum and tropical cocktails set against a modern, spacious backdrop in the heart of Midtown.

Death & Taxes is a dark and intimate cocktail lounge with an apothecary aesthetic specializing in rare and sought-after whiskeys. You'll find fresh artisanal cocktails made with seasonal ingredients, house-made syrups, and infusions.

1864 is a corner bar awash in Victorian accoutrements. You can collapse in one of many velvet fainting couches while sipping a lavender lemon drop in the shadow of a portrait of President Lincoln, who was instrumental in making Nevada a state. Hello, 1864—the Civil War called, and it wants its bar back.

Rum Sugar Lime
1039 S Virginia St., 775-384-1024
rumsugarlime.com

1864 Tavern
290 California Ave., 775-329-1864
1864tavern.com

Death & Taxes Provisions and Spirits
26 Cheney St., 775-324-2630
deathandtaxesreno.com

TIP

For a legendary destination bar in Reno that mixes fire and water, visit the Peppermill's Fireside Lounge, which opened more than four decades ago as part of the original Peppermill Inn Coffee Shop & Lounge. The Fireside offers plush couches, dim lighting, and an iconic firepit, plus intimate enclaves to enjoy a romantic cocktail.

2707 S Virginia St., 775-826-2121
peppermillreno.com/nightlife

COMMEMORATE A SPECIAL OCCASION
AT BRICKS RESTAURANT

Celebrating something spectacular—even if it's just surviving another day ending in "y"? Here are several must-visits:

You'll feel like you stepped back in time when you walk into Bricks, its exposed brick (as implied by the name) and intimate, dimly lit interior paying homage to classically appointed fine-dining establishments. Yet its timeless take on contemporary American cuisine makes it a classic option for any special occasion. Their newest dining environment, a beautiful courtyard, is perfection on a warm Northern Nevada evening.

Also boasting a charming patio, Lulou's is the perfect upscale date-night destination. The flavors showcase the highest quality ingredients, which are fresh and local, with their menu changing seasonally. Here's hoping you're there on a night featuring butterscotch pudding for dessert—this one's worth the calories!

When you walk through the doors at Mario's Portofino, it's like you're transporting to old-school Europe, with chef creations that are authentically Italian. And the welcoming ambiance extends to service as well, as you'll feel like you're a member of their extended family. Bonus: They're open for lunch!

Bricks Restaurant and Wine Bar
1695 S Virginia St., 775-786-2277
bricksrestaurant.com

Lulou's
1470 S Virginia St., 775-329-9979

Mario's Portofino
1505 S Virginia St., 775-825-7779
mariosportofino.com

25

DINE ALFRESCO
AT DAVID'S GRILL

Featuring abundant sunshine more than 300 days every year, Northern Nevada has its fair share of gorgeous outdoor dining options. Here are two bright spots:

Overlooking the scenic Red Hawk Golf Course, David's Grill has an expansive patio and live music seasonally. It feels a bit like Lake Tahoe dining, without the lake: sunsets are particularly breathtaking, and you'll often see a variety of wildlife—including the golf course's namesake red hawks. Don't miss favorites such as a fresh ahi tuna salad with a light, bright ginger vinaigrette; exceptional waffle-cut fries; and a decadent white chocolate bread pudding.

If "waterfront dining" and "Sparks, Nevada" don't seem to entirely go together, you haven't visited the Sparks Marina—which is a recreational area featuring a 2.5-mile walking path, fishing, and boating. Overlooking the marina is Sparks Water Bar, with the same owners as Gar Woods—a hugely popular Lake Tahoe restaurant. That means you get to enjoy a world-famous Wet Woody (Gar Woods signature cocktail) while dining on soups, burgers, or entrees.

David's Grill
6600 N Wingfield Pkwy., Sparks
775-626-1000
redhawkgolfandresort.com/dining

Sparks Water Bar
325 Harbour Cove Dr., Sparks
775-351-1500
sparkswaterbar.com

26

GO OFF THE EATEN PATH
AT PIETRO'S FAMIGLIA

Foodie destinations in Northern Nevada tend to cluster around certain regions, but that doesn't mean exploration is futile. A few are a bit harder to find, but well worth the effort.

In downtown Sparks, you'll need to look up to find this hidden hot spot. Travel up a set of stairs to transport yourself to a secret hideaway known as Pietro's Famiglia Ristorante Italiano. While specials change nightly, you can count on authentic Italian cuisine and an unmatched tiramisu. This is a special date-night destination, especially on weekends as you're serenaded by live music while enjoying your linguini or lasagna.

Another restaurant that's not quite downtown and not quite Midtown is tucked into a corner on Plumb Lane bordering the city's Old Southwest. The Kitchen Table has an open-kitchen concept with a warm and welcoming vibe to match. Contemporary Italian dishes adorn the menu, which changes seasonally. Make a reservation, sit on the patio during warmer months, and bring cash, as this restaurant charges a credit card fee.

Pietro's Famiglia Ristorante Italiano
834 Victorian Ave., Ste. 200, Sparks, 775-355-7557
pietrosfamiglia.com

The Kitchen Table
530 W Plumb Ln., Ste. A, 775-384-3959
thekitchentablereno.com

MAKE GOOD CHOICES
AT GREAT FULL GARDENS

Enjoying a guilt-free restaurant experience can feel like a rarity, as "tasty" is often code for "indulgent." But that's far from the case at these destinations.

First up, we have Great Full Gardens. The name itself implies the benefits—you'll eat many of these dishes with your eyes first, plus they cater to dietary lifestyles such as paleo, gluten-free, vegan, and organic. So satisfy your cravings for tasty kale (it does exist!) or an unparalleled grilled portobello sandwich—plus clean, healthful soups from Gino the Soup Man.

Next, travel to California (Avenue—or the state, as they also have a location in Mammoth) for a visit to Elixir Superfood & Juice. Their entire menu is 100 percent gluten-free, and they use organic whole-food ingredients, no GMOs, no preservatives, and no refined sugars. They serve a variety of warm grain bowls (highly recommend the Patagonia), salads, smoothies, and cold-pressed juice. Definitely splurge a little by trying the tahini chocolate chip cookie!

Great Full Gardens
Multiple locations throughout Reno/Sparks
greatfullgardens.com

Elixir Superfood & Juice
24 California Ave., 775-622-8368
enjoyelixir.com

28

TREAT YOURSELF TO TACOS AND TEQUILA AT MARI CHUY'S

For a truly elevated sampling of delightful Mexican cuisine, you can't go wrong with these delectable destinations:

Mari Chuy's is a mashup on many levels. Married owners Mari and Chuy make up the name, creating legendary fare at four local restaurants. In Midtown and Sparks, it's a fresh Mex experience . . . with a side of margaritas; at the Rancharrah location, it's all about the botanas (Mexican small plates) and tequila, with more than 100 artisan tequilas that are 100 percent blue agave. Be sure to visit them all to experience their individual personalities, but the common denominator at Mari Chuy's is all about the personal touch.

Mexcal's menu is made for mixing and matching, with "avenue tacos" (maybe because they're a skosh classier than a street?) including their house specialty: *quesabirria*—braised short rib, cheese, onions, and cilantro. Order an avenue taco or two, a *bocadillo* (appetizer) of guac or ahi ceviche, and top it off with a tour of tequila favorites.

Mari Chuy's
Locations in Midtown, Rancharrah, Sparks, and airport, 775-322-6866
marichuys.com

Mexcal
516 S Virginia St., 775-433-1080
mexcalreno.com

29

DON'T WORRY, BE AT HAPPY HOUR
AT BISTRO NAPA

On any given weekday between 4 and 6 p.m., Reno foodies leave the office and beeline for these destinations:

On the second floor of the Atlantis, enthusiastic happy hourers wait in clusters outside the gates of Bistro Napa well before opening. Arrive early, as seats fill up fast for the half-price small plates (including fresh oysters and flatbreads), specialty craft cocktails, and 40 premium wines by the glass.

In downtown Reno, Liberty Food & Wine Exchange features fabulous prices on their scrumptious small plates, draft beer, house wine, and well drinks. The Liberty Fondue with brioche pretzel twists and apples is a must-try!

Washoe Public House offers generously portioned $6 small plates, such as a cup of soup and half a grilled cheese or half an order of Irish nachos. Accompany your bites with half-price beer, wine, and well drinks.

Bistro Napa
Atlantis Casino Resort Spa
3800 S Virginia St., 775-335-4539
atlantiscasino.com/reno-restaurants/bistro-napa

Liberty Food & Wine Exchange
100 N Sierra St., 775-336-1091
libertyfoodandwine.com

Washoe Public House
275 Hill St., 775-322-2710
washoepublichouse.com

30

FEED YOUR SOUL (AND APPETITE)
AT PINOCCHIO'S

There's no shortage of big hearts among Northern Nevada's foodie community. Here's just one example of a local establishment using fabulous food plus a fun atmosphere to effect change.

Pinocchio is an eclectic local restaurant with two locations that are literal and figurative feasts—for the stomach and the eyes. The walls and ceiling are a cacophony of random objects including skis, marionettes, and vintage signs. Order a classic menu item such as the parmesan-crusted chicken, and then engage your server in a chat about their annual Moms on the Run event. Since 1999, Pinocchio's Moms on the Run has provided financial support to Northern Nevada women diagnosed with breast or gynecological cancer.

Owner JP Pinocchio and his wife, Barbara, started the goofy Mother's Day run (costumes encouraged!) in 1999 to honor Barbara's sister, Debra, who died of breast cancer. To date, they've raised more than $6.5 million, benefiting 5,500 women along the way. Pinocchio's is all about great food, community spirit, and giving back—talk about putting your money where your mouth is!

Pinocchio's
5995 S Virginia St., 775-826-5151
4820 Vista Blvd., Sparks
775-626-0101
pinocchiosbarandgrill.com

TIP

Want to enjoy a glass of wine, a beer, or a latte—and adopt a cat while you're at it? Reno's got you covered at the Enchanted Cat Café. This unique spot has partnered with local cat rescues, allowing you to hang out for an hourly rate among numerous roaming felines. Purr-fection!

8555 Double R Blvd., Ste. 104, 775-418-9700
enchantedcatcafe.com

Great Reno Balloon Races

MUSIC AND ENTERTAINMENT

31

DANCE, DINE, AND DISCOVER
AT RENO PUBLIC MARKET

While this is the first entry in the "Music and Entertainment" category, Reno Public Market could easily reside in any category. It's an entertainment venue, a dining hall, an artist collective, and a shopping destination. It's also a vibe—with roll-up windows welcoming in the balmy outdoors, lofty ceilings, abundant glass overlooking the Sierra, and space to shop, connect, and explore.

Once a retail property in Reno called Shopper's Square, this new concept marries history, culture, and fun. The centerpiece is an elevated stage under the purple neon glow of the name "Faye's," a meaningful nod to the past: Faye's was a boutique lingerie store from the 1960s, and construction crews discovered the original sign while peeling back layers of the building. Now the "Live at Faye's" stage hosts musicians, comedians, authors, children's groups, movie screenings, and trivia competitions.

While you're enjoying onstage entertainment or watching the game, you'll partake in bites and beverages prepared by top culinary creators from the expansive food hall. Don't forget to pause and shop for items created by locals in surrounding retail spaces.

299 E Plumb Ln., 775-993-3220
renopublicmarket.com

32

MEANDER DOWN MUSICAL MEMORY LANE

AT RECYCLED RECORDS

Sometimes, you just need a good ol' throwback record store experience. And while those can prove elusive, not so in Reno: Recycled Records is your go-to destination if you're craving the authentic sounds of vinyl for your classic home turntable setup.

Despite the name, it's about more than "just" records (though they have about 50,000 of those): CDs (in the market for some Springsteen or Smiths?), cassettes (no mix tapes, but there's abundant fodder here), and even some eight-tracks and reel-to-reels can be found among the treasures.

They'll even buy from and/or trade with you, by appointment—just in case you still have a shoebox full of gems. They're also HUGE supporters of local musicians, so be sure to ask about upcoming shows or merch.

As the name implies, this is a secondhand retail music store, but what the name doesn't reveal is the store's longevity: Recycled Records has been a go-to destination for music lovers since 1978. The staff is knowledgeable, and the store has a natural funky vibe. And the smell? Well, it's a lot like teen spirit.

4048 Kietzke Ln., 775-826-4119
recrecreno.com

33

GRAB YOUR QUARTERS
AND PRESS START

When you think "Centipede," you can feel it, right?—the smooth rolly ball, the dimpled button, the sound of the falling fleas leaving trails of fresh mushrooms. Retro games are cool again, meaning retro arcades are back and better than ever. And when I say "better," I mean—they serve beer and wine!

Press Start is one of those locations, with throwback arcade options, pinball, air hockey, and a full bar menu with craft beer and cocktails. Kids are welcome until 7 p.m.

If you're looking for more of an adults-only vibe, head to Playfield 76. This location is a classic arcade, elevated—featuring shareable snacks, pizzas, and an extensive bar.

Want more of an analog vibe? Visit the Glass Die for board game + bar fun. It's adults-only here too, so grab a beer, and check out any of their 1,000 board games.

Press Start
600 S Center St., 775-657-9981
renopressstart.com

Playfield 76
150 N Arlington Ave., 775-384-2564
playfield76.com

The Glass Die
675 Holcomb Ave., 775-384-1456
theglassdie.com

34

TAKE A TRIP TO ARTOWN
DURING JULY AND BEYOND

When Artown began in 1996, it attracted 30,000 guests to arts and music events for three weeks in July. Now almost three decades later, the National Endowment for the Arts considers it one of the most comprehensive arts festivals in the country, and the festival spans the entire month—and then some!

Intended as a way to strengthen Reno's arts community, Artown now annually fills a calendar with about 600 multidisciplinary events in more than 100 locations citywide. Past headlining acts have included Mikhail Baryshnikov, India.Arie, the American Ballet Theatre, and Michael Bublé, and local artists are featured in a variety of performances as well.

Workshops, dance, film, theater, art walks, and kids' programming are all part of the mix. Event highlights include headliner performances on opening and closing nights, a world music series, and movies in the park. And if you're not visiting during July, look for Artown's Encore Series—live events from high-caliber performing artists during non-Artown months.

Best of all, most Artown events are free or low cost.

775-322-1538
artown.org

35

MAKE IT A DREAMY MIDSUMMER NIGHT

WITH THE LAKE TAHOE SHAKESPEARE FESTIVAL

In terms of entertainment, one of the most unique experiences in the area involves late midsummer evenings, Shakespeare, lake views, stars, and sand. The Lake Tahoe Shakespeare Festival marries all these concepts perfectly, inviting audiences to watch a work of the Bard—alternating nights with a more modern play—on an outdoor stage resting along the shores of Lake Tahoe. The viewers, sitting in outdoor lounge chairs under blankets brought from home, can run their toes through the sand, sip a glass of wine, and chat with friends during intermission.

The acclaimed festival is usually raucous, always well-attended, and abundantly fun. Dates vary, but the festival typically falls in midsummer for about seven weeks total, seven nights a week. The natural sand amphitheater overlooking Lake Tahoe provides awe-inspiring views before the sun goes down, and after, actors on stage vie for your attention, competing with the majestic starry skies above.

Bring a flashlight, dress in layers, and be prepared for a night of unparalleled views and Shakespearean fun.

Nevada's Sand Harbor State Park, Lake Tahoe
2005 Hwy. 28, Incline Village, 1-800-747-4697
laketahoeshakespeare.com

36

ORDER A HEAPING HELPING OF SOUL

AT NASHVILLE SOCIAL CLUB

Who knew you could discover the sounds of Nashville in the heart of Northern Nevada? Our state's capital city is home to Nashville Social Club, a venue celebrating "Americana Roots" music—from folk to blues, country to bluegrass, gospel to rock, and a little jazz thrown in for good measure.

Two stages are home to intimate, up-close-and-personal live music performances—the Swan Music Hall, with national and local artists, as well as the Soft Note Stage, featuring mostly free concerts. And don't miss the chance to strut your stuff (or learn with the masses) during their honkey-tonk–style line and country dance nights.

Best of all, if you work up an appetite before or after all that singing and dancing, Nashville Social Club is a full-service restaurant featuring hip southern cuisine. Of course, they have the classic down-home chicken and waffles combo, as well as shrimp and grits, but they also serve salads, brick-oven pizzas, burgers, and biscuits.

With a made-for-each-other mix of magnificent music and fabulous food, you'll feed your soul—and your stomach—at Nashville Social Club.

1105 S Carson St., Carson City, 775-515-0020
thenashvilleclub.com

37

LAY YOUR EYES ON THE SKIES

AT THE GREAT RENO BALLOON RACES

A mosaic of floating balloons is the colorful paint and Reno's brilliant skies are the canvas during the annual Great Reno Balloon Race—the largest free hot-air ballooning event in the world.

During three days in early September, you can look up at sunrise from just about any corner of the region to see about 100 hot-air balloons dotting the tranquil horizon. Many locals remember the event's modest beginnings in 1982, when just a few hundred spectators watched 20 balloons launch from Rancho San Rafael Park. But now, the Great Reno Balloon Race has reached lofty new heights with scores more balloons, abundant food and entertainment options, and 100,000-plus visitors and neighbors taking it all in.

Arrive predawn for the stained-glass effect of Dawn Patrol and the Glow Show, bring some cocoa and blankets, and be prepared for your spirit to take flight.

Rancho San Rafael Park
1595 N Sierra St., 775-391-8562
renoballoon.com

MEET THE GOLDEN TURTLE:
RENO'S PIONEER CENTER

If you're traveling south from the Reno arch down Virginia Street, you can't miss a resplendent, somewhat retro-looking dome as you transition from downtown to Midtown. Under this roof is Reno's Pioneer Center for the Performing Arts, built in 1967, its gold-anodized aluminum geodesic dome comprised of 500 interlocking panels glistening in the sun. Inside, the orchestra level of the theater is depressed below ground level, allowing the roof to nearly touch the ground at the corners.

Locals lovingly refer to the building—named to national, state, and city historic registers—as the "golden turtle." But the real name captures the spirit of the pioneer family sculpture looking westward to the Sierra Nevada range, created in 1939 and called "Humanity."

The structure is one of Reno's iconic cultural touchstones, with 1,500 seats from which you can watch performances by the Reno Philharmonic, A.V.A. Ballet Theatre, and Artown. It's also home to Broadway Comes to Reno, which has been bringing touring Broadway shows to Reno for decades.

100 S Virginia St., 775-686-6600, or tickets by phone: 775-434-1050
pioneercenter.com

REVEL IN BIG DRAMA
AT RENO LITTLE THEATER

Reno's theater scene is scrappy, fun, and overflowing with local talent. Catch a performance at any of Reno's venues—but remember, they often sell out, so grab your tickets early.

Reno Little Theater is Nevada's longest-running community theater and features musicals, comedy, mystery, suspense, and drama. Recurring performances include the monthly Sunday jazz at RLT; monthly senior readers' theater with Ageless Repertory Theater; and regular performances by Latino Arte and Culture.

Brüka Theatre is a performance art space in the downtown arts district devoted to classic, contemporary, and original productions for both child and adult audiences. It's known for staging innovative works with talented performers and an acclaimed Theatre for Children series.

Good Luck Macbeth typically stages six productions a year—both original and classic works—with additional smaller theatrical events, along with Reno Jazz Orchestra concerts and other community events.

Reno Little Theater
147 E Pueblo St., 775-813-8900
renolittletheater.org

Brüka
99 N Virginia St., 775-323-3221
bruka.org

Good Luck Macbeth
124 W Taylor St., 775-322-3716
goodluckmacbeth.org

YES, AND . . . YOU CAN PLAY, TOO!

Interested in testing out your own acting chops? Try your hand at Reno Improv. This is a safe, welcoming space where improvisation skills are creatively coached, and fun is had by all. You'll meet new people, plus learning improv techniques can improve your communication skills and self-confidence.

Sign up for a weekly "playground" beginners' workshop, take a class, or attend a performance to see what all the buzz is about!

Reno Improv
695 Willow St., 775-462-6841
renoimprov.org

GET A HEAPING DOSE OF CULTURE
FROM THE RENO PHIL

To say Reno is a breeding ground for musical talent is an understatement—with a robust music program at the University of Nevada, Reno, and nationally recognized performing arts venues, opportunities abound for musicians in the Biggest Little City. So take any opportunity to grab tickets for local choirs and orchestras, including these:

The Reno Phil performs for more than 50,000 people annually through a full season of concerts featuring internationally acclaimed guest artists and works by legendary and living composers. It consists of an orchestra, chorus, and youth chorus.

Reno Chamber Orchestra performs intimate musical experiences through its orchestra and ensembles. Performances often take place on campus at UNR and the historic Trinity Episcopal Cathedral.

The Reno Pops Orchestra is composed of students and adults of all ages. They perform free and low-cost concerts at various venues in Northern Nevada and routinely offer themed and holiday performances.

Reno Phil
Performing at various locations, 775-323-6393
renophil.com

Reno Chamber Orchestra
Performing at various locations, 775-348-9413
renochamberorchestra.org

Reno Pops Orchestra
Performing at various locations, 775-673-1234
renopops.org

GO UNDERGROUND FOR ENTERTAINMENT

IN THE BASEMENT

This is certainly not the dusty, probably haunted basement of your childhood home. Instead, it's an unexpected underground entertainment and shopping experience situated beneath the historic 1932 US Post Office in downtown Reno.

The best time to journey down to The Basement may be Third Saturdays: starting at 10 a.m., The Basement hosts the monthly "Rush the River" event that features live entertainment, pop-ups, a makers market, and food. Then take time to wander around The Basement's local marketplace of unique merchants.

As you explore, be sure to take in the Art Deco/Moderne style of the historic building—originally designed by Nevada's preeminent architect, Frederic J. DeLongchamps—which was listed in the National Register of Historic Places in 1990.

Everyone knows basements house the best-kept secrets; Reno's best-kept secret may just be The Basement itself!

50 S Virginia St., 775-771-0334
thebasementreno.com

WALK ON WATER
AT LEX NIGHTCLUB

Reno typically rejects comparisons to Las Vegas, but there's one destination that perhaps rivals even the splashiest spot offered by our shiny sister down south: LEX Nightclub, tucked inside the Grand Sierra Resort. Once inside this high-energy nightlife venue, you'll be greeted by a sea of skin, screens, scaffolding, and glowsticks, as popular DJs and headliners ignite the stage.

Nine intricate skylights and a $2 million lighting system provide an impressive backdrop to the club's 25,000 square feet of space, highlighted by an indoor pool that is partially covered by a glass dance floor—creating the illusion of dancing on water.

LEX features three full bars, 33 VIP tables, and top-notch amenities. Just remember to follow the "upscale fashionable" dress code, and check the website before you visit to ensure your 'fit complies with a list of attire and accessories that are not permitted as well. (Translation: leave the beanies and ripped clothing at home, you party animals.)

Grand Sierra Resort and Casino
2500 E 2nd St., 775-789-5399
lexnightclub.com

43

FUEL A CREATIVE SPARK
AT THE HOLLAND PROJECT

Reno certainly nurtures its community of creators, and one of the most vibrant hotbeds of local performance art is the Holland Project. This all-ages arts and music initiative by young people, for young people (or just those young at heart) provides access to music, art, workshops, and community service and activism.

The Holland Stage hosts an extensive roster of DJs, karaoke nights, touring bands, exhibitions, and beyond. Check their website for a calendar—they typically produce more than 200 arts-focused programs each year.

A recurring offering is Holland's Billboard Gallery, which showcases the work of exceptional emerging and established regional artists on billboards throughout Reno's surface streets. Find locations (with directions) on their website.

The Holland Project's intimate, chill venue emits an urban vibe and is welcome to people of all ages. Catch a glimpse of the next generation of performance art and creative talent at an upcoming Holland event, or tune into 97.7 KWNK—its volunteer-run, member-supported community radio station.

140 Vesta St., 775-742-1858
hollandreno.org

44

EXPLORE THE SOUTH 40

AT THIS SOUTH RENO HOT SPOT

Family fun is in focus at South 40, an entertainment and food utopia in Reno's South Meadows neighborhood.

While kids can spend hours in the state-of-the-art arcade complete with virtual reality headsets, classic claw games, Skee-Ball, and more, parents can play too—their setting an indoor backyard featuring a dedicated bar, corn hole, bowling, axe-throwing, a stage for live music, six TVs, and a big-screen projector.

Live music is on stage every weekend, so check the website for a calendar of upcoming acts. You'll encounter everything from acoustic sets to comedy, blues to soft rock, paint-and-sip parties to beer pong tournaments.

All that play is guaranteed to build up an appetite. Lucky for you, the menu at South 40 reads like a sophisticated block party, with wagyu sliders, pizza, ribs, and steak among the offerings. It may sound counterintuitive, but the quick-seared sesame-crusted ahi appetizer with carrot salad, pickled ginger, and sesame soy sauce is a must-try.

1445 S Meadows Pkwy., 775-800-9070
south-40-reno.com

45

GET AMP-ED
AT THE BREWERY ARTS CENTER

Carson City's arts and entertainment renaissance has been bolstered by a confluence of factors, but perhaps spearheaded by the efforts of the Brewery Arts Center (BAC). As the BAC's centerpiece annual event, the Levitt AMP Carson City Music Series has energized massive audiences and reenergized a historic portion of Nevada's state capital.

The free Levitt AMP concerts (the acronym translating to "Amplify, Music, Places") have been grant-funded since 2016 and are continuing into the future, with the grant awarded to cities transforming underused public spaces into thriving destinations. Since 2016, more than 30,000 attendees experience the power of live music annually along a once-forgotten Carson City corridor. The series spans summer months, bringing big-name bands and diverse sounds to locals and visitors alike.

But the BAC is more than AMP: its campus encompasses two city blocks, has three performance facilities, and hosts multiple concerts and workshops throughout the year.

All of this makes the historic Brewery Arts Center—during, before, or after the Levitt AMP concert series—a must-experience destination.

449 W King St., Carson City, 775-883-1976
breweryarts.org

DELIGHT IN MUSIC AND MARTINIS

AT ROXY'S PIANO BAR

On the second level of Eldorado Resort Casino is a sprawling, 20-piece fountain. It's appropriately named the Fountain of Fortune, considering it sits practically at the intersection of two of the three casinos that make up what's known as THE ROW—with its 227,000 square feet of casino space.

And overlooking that fountain is Roxy's Bar and Lounge. How fortunate, indeed.

Roxy's is a place to sip and be seen, with its live piano and vocals that serve as the ultimate sensory backdrop. The music is either the reason you've come, or it's the cherry on top (or more appropriately, skewered olive inside) of the pièce de résistance: the drink in your hand. Roxy's is famous for its menu of 102 martinis and a selection of 350 wines.

So sip a Dean Martini as you lounge in an overstuffed leather chair, bask in the glow of the Fountain of Fortune, and watch as the ivories are gloriously tickled on Roxy's grand piano.

Eldorado at THE ROW
345 N Virginia St., 800-879-8879
caesars.com/eldorado-reno

Red Hawk Golf Course

SPORTS AND RECREATION

CLIMB THE WALLS
AT WHITNEY PEAK'S BASECAMP

If you're looking for something to get the adrenaline pumping, consider a visit to Whitney Peak's BaseCamp. This destination is a celebration of climbing and fitness that occupies the entire second floor of the nongaming, nonsmoking boutique hotel in downtown Reno.

A 7,000-square-foot indoor bouldering park with a slackline, dedicated kids' room, cave area, and various rings and ropes are featured indoors. But the part of the experience that will keep you talking is the outdoor rock wall, which at 164 feet is the world's tallest artificial climbing wall, as certified by Guinness World Records.

Locals often challenge their guests to experience the best view of our iconic Reno arch—from the tippy top of the wall. You'll be scaling the side of a 16-story major hotel, in the heart of downtown Reno, above the city's main thoroughfare and most identifiable landmark.

No biggie.

255 N Virginia St., 775-398-5443
basecampreno.com

48

SWING FOR THE FENCES
WITH SOME GOOD OL' FASHIONED ACEBALL

Baseball season in Northern Nevada is perhaps our favorite time of the year. On any given game day, you'll find us at the park, drinking a beer and watching our hometown minor league team: the Reno Aces.

The Triple-A affiliate of the Arizona Diamondbacks plays at Greater Nevada Field in the heart of Reno, a destination that has spurred its own retail and nightlife neighborhood called the Freight House District. Watch a game, and then visit one of the many surrounding bars and clubs for a taste of after-hours fun.

A few tips: avoid the mascot tongue at all costs (it's a truly terrifying sight and rivals the gesticulations of Gene Simmons); watch the scoreboard during the seventh-inning stretch; encourage your kids to run the bases at game-end if given the option; and aim to attend on a night with fireworks, which usually happens on weekends.

Play ball!

Greater Nevada Field
250 Evans Ave., 775-334-7000
renoaces.com

49

TAKE A HIKE—LITERALLY—
ALONG HUNTER CREEK TRAIL

Northern Nevada's high-desert terrain creates the ideal landscape for hikers who enjoy rocks, sagebrush, evergreens, water features, and everything in between. It's practically impossible to mention all the incredible hiking trails in and around Reno, so here we'll note two local favorites: Hunter Creek Trail and Galena.

Hunter Creek Trail is more a locals' secret—or at least so lore suggests, though the trail can get very busy. Go early for the most solitude; also note that the trail is mostly in sun, which can be brutal in summer. However, the payoff—about three miles up—is superb: Hunter Creek Falls, flanked by rocky banks and verdant hillsides.

Galena Canyon, south of town, contains diverse trails for every aptitude level. About seven different nature trails comprise the well-mapped system, with brochures and signposts available to tell you about the ecology and cultural history of the area.

Hunter Creek Trail
Trailhead on Woodchuck Cir. in west Reno, 775-331-6444
travelnevada.com/hiking/hunter-creek-trail

Galena Creek Visitor Center
18250 Mt. Rose Hwy., 775-849-4948
galenacreekvisitorcenter.org

DID YOU KNOW?

More than 80 percent of Nevada is public land—the highest percentage among all states.

So whether you're biking, hiking, walking, riding, skiing, rock climbing, or snowmobiling, you'll need maps to guide you toward and around Nevada's abundant trails. Nevada Trail Finder is a one-stop resource for trails statewide, connecting you to current information and maps about four-season outdoor opportunities and providing tools to track your trail adventures.

The free website features more than 88,000 miles of motorized and 6,800 miles of nonmotorized trails throughout Nevada.

nvtrailfinder.com

50

HAVE A TUBE-ULAR TIME

FLOATING THE TRUCKEE

The Truckee River is the ultimate aquatic playground for outdoor enthusiasts, but just because you love adventure doesn't mean you're constantly looking for the extremes. So during those seasons when the weather is warm and the Truckee River has ample water, tubing is a relatively relaxing endeavor—with a little adrenaline thrown in for good measure.

You'll see wildlife in the water and along the shores as you float/paddle, observe abundant changes in ecology, and even view a line of historic Reno mansions along the way.

Some companies, such as Sierra Adventures, will rent you sturdy inner tubes, life jackets, and helmets—and even give you an upstream lift in a shuttle.

From your put-in location, it's between a two- and four-hour float back down to the Whitewater Park, depending on your point of origin. Keep in mind that you'll be floating in full sun, which can be a bit exhausting: bring a hat and sunglasses, water to drink, and tie a dry bag to your tube for any personal items.

Sierra Adventures
11 N Sierra St., Ste. 101, 775-323-8928 or toll-free 866-323-8928
wildsierra.com

51

SAFELY SEEK OUT
RENO'S ABUNDANT WILD HORSES

Often resembling small grazing dots along the hillsides surrounding Reno—and even venturing into suburban neighborhoods—wild horses are popular and revered in Northern Nevada. To see a horse in the wild is an unforgettable experience, harkening back to images of the Wild West in centuries past. Many locations in and around town are hotbeds for wild horse sightings—from Damonte Ranch to Hidden Valley, Washoe Valley to the Virginia City foothills, and beyond.

One way to experience this natural wonder is to take an ecotourism adventure in search of mustangs, scouring foothills and remote passages where equine families commonly band together. Your tour guides, like those from Sonny Boys Tours, will provide insights about the free-roaming wild horses of the West, filling your time together with compelling stories and facts that add depth to the experience.

Whichever option you choose—DIY or guided—take some time to explore the surrounding desert landscape to try to find a horse in the wild. But respect their space, as these majestic animals are to be seen but not touched.

Sonny Boys Tours
775-200-5205
renowildhorsetours.com

52

HOWL IN SUPPORT
OF THE NEVADA WOLF PACK

Reno is a college town through and through, which means you'll encounter rabid fans on game day, flying Wolf Pack flags, dressed in silver and blue, and battling for prime parking places around campus.

There's fun to be had at every meet, game, and competition—from catching a baseball at Peccole Park to watching the Pack shoot hoops at Lawlor Events Center to cheering on a blitz in an intense clash over pigskin at Mackay Stadium, which sits high on the hill overlooking the campus.

But that's not all, obviously. Regardless of the season, you'll likely find a sport and a game to watch—soccer, tennis, swimming, diving, and many more. Attending a University of Nevada, Reno, sports event is a uniquely Northern Nevada experience, one that brings out the Pack Pride in all of us.

Various Reno locations
nevadawolfpack.com

CYCLE, HIKE, RUN, OR WALK

THE TAHOE-PYRAMID TRAIL

While it's common for cities to figuratively spring from (or around) water, it's fairly uncommon for a river to define a region as clearly as the Truckee River defines our area. The river starts in Lake Tahoe, the Truckee being Tahoe's only significant outlet, and it travels downstream 121 miles to Pyramid Lake.

An interesting journey is to follow the Truckee River—using a bicycle or your feet. It begins at Lake Tahoe Dam near Tahoe City and meanders from there through the quaint town of Truckee, which is only 30 minutes from Reno.

From Truckee, it mostly follows the I-80 corridor, turning sharply east to leave California and find its home in Nevada, where it snakes through Reno and Sparks. Ultimately, it terminates at striking Pyramid Lake, a remnant of prehistoric Lake Lahontan on the Pyramid Lake Paiute Tribe Reservation.

The Tahoe-Pyramid Trail bikeway has been under construction for two decades and is close to completion. Use their website to get trail info, download maps, and learn all the tips to undertake this grand adventure.

Tahoe-Pyramid Trail
775-825-9868
tahoepyramidtrail.org

54

APPLY THE 10 PERCENT RULE

AT LAKERIDGE GOLF COURSE

Did you know that Reno is scientifically made for better golfing? True facts: At our altitude and according to the laws of golf ball aerodynamics, players realize about a 10 percent gain in yardage. It's something about the dry air robbing each ball's tiny dimples of moisture, meaning they're lighter and go farther—or so we've been told by those studying the moisture content of tiny golf ball dimples.

Within 90 minutes of Reno, you'll find more than 50 courses where the 10 percent rule applies. And it seems our reputation precedes us, as we're home to the PGA's Barracuda Championship Golf Tournament, and Edgewood Tahoe Golf Course hosts the star-studded American Century Celebrity Golf Championship each July.

Here's one more bit of inspiration: Local golfing lore is all about the 15th hole of LakeRidge Golf Course. Robert Trent Jones Sr. designed the course, including this iconic hole, whose tee sits 145 feet above a 239-yard hole on a natural island green. It's a world-famous par 3, and it's begging for you to conquer it.

Barracuda Championship
barracudachampionship.com

American Century Celebrity Golf Championship
americancenturychampionship.com

LakeRidge Golf Course
1218 Golf Club Dr., 775-825-2200
lakeridgegolfcourse.com

55

GET STARSTRUCK
AT LAKE TAHOE

Light pollution makes stargazing in the Truckee Meadows difficult, but one only needs to head to the hills to find locations where the stars will spread before you like fireflies swarming in the night sky.

With clear skies happening about 300 days per year in the area, Lake Tahoe proves the ultimate location for celestial viewing. So pack your telescope, binoculars, cocoa, and blankets, and check out these (among other) prime locations.

Slide Mountain
Mt. Rose-Ski Tahoe Winters Creek Lodge Parking Lot:
breathtaking views overlooking Washoe Lake

Nevada Beach
(US Hwy. 50, Round Hill): endless open beach and sky views

Monitor Pass
(Hwy. 395, 2.5 miles south of the Nevada state line, then take Hwy. 89 W toward Markleeville): an overlook with dramatic sky and lake vistas

TAKE A DEEP DIVE INTO HISTORY
AT BOWERS MANSION

Pack a picnic lunch and take a trip through time to the Victorian era at Bowers Mansion Regional Park, situated between Reno and Carson City in North Washoe Valley. The lush greens surrounding the mansion are perfect spots for a blanket and some quiet contemplative time, while the kids (and kids at heart) can soak up some fun in the pool.

Located right next to the historic mansion, this fun, Z-shaped, 44-meter outdoor pool is heated by a natural hot spring. A wading pool is also available for small children.

On the grounds, you'll find children's play areas and abundant places to explore—including a hiking trail leading to the Bowers family gravesite. You can also tour the mansion for a sneak peek into the posh life of the home's original owners, Comstock millionaires Eilley and Sandy Bowers. The home was constructed in 1863, after the Bowers struck it rich staking a claim in the aptly named Gold Hill.

4005 Old US 395 N, North Washoe Valley, 775-849-0201
travelnevada.com/historical-interests/bowers-mansion

57

LIVE THE FAIRY TALE
AT CHICKADEE RIDGE

You know that scene in Cinderella—or is it Snow White (or both?)—where birds delicately land on the princess's outstretched finger? Totally fiction, right? Nope—this is a common occurrence at Chickadee Ridge, overlooking Lake Tahoe. The ridge rises above Tahoe Meadows, just southwest of Mount Rose. It's a fairly easy, two-mile-ish climb with a beautiful payoff: views from the summit reveal the splendor of Lake Tahoe and the mountains to the west.

Chickadee Ridge is thusly named because of the prevalence of the adorable tiny birds who hang out in the lodgepole and whitebark pines on the ridge. As promised, they'll eat wild birdseed you bring from home directly from your hand. (Quick tip: based on personal experience, these tiny avian divas literally pick around to find the black oil sunflower seeds, so make sure those are in the mix you bring with you.)

Tiny diva birds, eating right from your hand. Just like Cinderella . . . or was it Mary Poppins?

Accessed via the Mount Rose Highway (SR 431)
Tahoe Meadows parking is one mile past the Mount Rose Summit

PLAY LIKE A KID
AT GRAND SIERRA RESORT

Most casino resorts are like giant playgrounds for adults, but perhaps nowhere is this truer than at Reno's Grand Sierra Resort (GSR). Want proof? You can do all of these at the GSR:

- Ice skate on Reno's only outdoor rink (seasonally available).
- Work on your driving game by aiming at eight floating island greens at the Grand Bay Driving Range.
- Perfect your blacklight bowling game.
- Drive super-fast on one of three go-kart tracks.
- Test your senses in Reno's newest immersive experience called Sensology (like an escape room, but catering to your five senses).
- Try your luck in four themed escape rooms.
- Participate in an immersive tethered virtual reality experience called Chaos Jump.
- Fasten yourself into a sling that hoists you 180 feet in the air, and then pull the ripcord to send yourself (yup, you're in control) on a mind-blowing descent that feels like free flying at 65 miles per hour.

Recreation? Yeah, just a few options here. Bring your resolve, and might we suggest carbo-loading beforehand?

2500 E 2nd St., 800-501-2651
grandsierraresort.com/activities

59

PACK SOME POLES (OR A BOARD), PICK A DIRECTION, AND HIT THE SLOPES

Of course, no book about Northern Nevada would be complete without mention of the region's winter sports of choice—skiing and boarding. Because when Lake Tahoe is in your backyard, snow is kinda your thing. The nice part is that Reno gets far less snow than they do at lake level, yet we can be on the slopes of more than a dozen ski/board/cross-country ski areas in most cases within an hour from home base.

The bottom line to all of this: You have options to consider. If you're looking for a destination for double black diamond runs, we've got it (but make good choices!). If you're a newbie just cutting your polar teeth, our resorts have abundant bunny hills. Or perhaps you're more interested in the aprés ski experience? No worries—we've got some cocoa, roaring fireplaces, and s'mores just waiting to be assembled.

Reno's location just a few miles from epic winter snowfalls makes it the perfect destination for skiing, snowboarding, sledding, snowshoeing, or however you choose to recreate in piles of fluffy white powder!

visitrenotahoe.com/ski

ENTER PEAK PARENTING MODE
AT WILD ISLAND

Let's face it, kids are hard work. But you know where they're surprisingly less hard? At a waterpark and 125,000-square-foot family entertainment center, obviously.

Of course, you'll still need to keep your eyes on them, but you certainly won't hear any complaints of boredom. The seasonal waterpark is a local favorite, with fast-moving lines often seen snaking down the stairs of the multiple daredevil water slides. The less adventurous can bob in the wave pool or float the lazy river. (Hot tip: guarantee a shady cool-down spot by renting a private cabana!)

Not so sunny out? No problem. Coconut Bowl is open 363 days a year (seriously!) and offers bowling, an interactive three-level play structure, indoor black-light mini golf, two outdoor mini-golf courses, a glowing electric go-kart track, laser tag, arcade games, pool tables, and more.

Exhausted yet? Go for an adventure in the wild and hear them proclaim, "Best. Parents. EVER!"

250 Wild Island Ct., Sparks, 775-359-2927
wildisland.com

61

KEEP YOUR EYES
ON THE SKIES

People who visit Reno are often struck by our clouds, which vary in size, texture, and density. This is all thanks to the Sierra Nevada, because as winds hit the range, air and moisture rise. This creates clouds that can resemble anything ranging from an alien invasion to Monet's pastel brushstrokes.

You don't even need to see the sun as it rises or sets to experience the majesty; the way dawn and dusk themselves change the textures and hues of the sky and the colors of the mountains are remarkable from pretty much any vantage point.

But here are a few local favorites:

- Rancho San Rafael Park, north Reno
- Emerald Bay, Lake Tahoe
- Pretty much any beach, Lake Tahoe
- Windy Hill, southwest Reno
- Donner Lake, CA
- The hills in east Sparks, notably on trails surrounding Wingfield Springs and Red Hawk

TRAVEL TO THE BUNDOX
FOR A BOCCE BALL BLAST

Nah, we kid. Unlike the common conception of "boondocks," this version is a place that's very close by—right in the middle of downtown Reno, in fact.

Bundox Bocce is a 22,000-square-foot indoor facility at the Renaissance Hotel and Spa. Talk about a place to play: here you'll find shuffleboard, ping pong, pool tables, arcade games, and a full bar with cocktails and snacks. The space also houses eight big-screen TVs and a spacious, dog-friendly patio.

But the real star of the show is bocce. Yes, *that* bocce—the game you've been playing during backyard barbecues has a home in Reno, and people are super serious about it . . . some even bring their own equipment! But if you're new to the sport, visit Bundox Bocce, let them set you up with your gear on one of seven indoor or two outdoor courts, and enjoy this game that's one-half bowling, one-half pool, and one-half croquet with a splash of mini golf thrown in. Sure, that equals more than a whole, but that just reflects the overabundance of fun you'll have playing bocce ball!

1 S Lake St., 775-321-5866
bundoxbocce.com

CHANNEL YOUR INNER LUMBERJACK AT RENO AXE

You know you're thinking it—is it really a good idea to combine hatchet-throwing with drinking? Well apparently it is, because axe-throwing is an activity that's becoming all the rage. And full disclosure: it's totally fun, stress-relieving, confidence-boosting, and empowering to boot! Axe-throwing—done in a safe environment, where you're first shown the ropes—is a great way to spend an hour or more with your friends.

Reno Axe and Social has the aforementioned safe space to practice your mad hatchet skills, as well as shuffleboard, ping pong, air hockey, darts, and pretty much any other way you can imagine adult playtime might look.

Axe & Throw offers axe sessions with a variety of digital targets in private, fully caged throwing lanes. As they describe it: "turbo-charged darts on steroids, or bowling for the adventurous." Sounds about right.

Smashin' Good Time is the place to let off that built-up steam, with a smash room for those looking for a more freestyle stress relief activity, or axe-throwing for a more targeted experience.

Reno Axe
100 N Sierra St., Ste. 105, 775-235-5658
renoaxe.com

Axe & Throw
Legends Sparks, 1180 Scheels Dr., Ste. B-109, 775-433-1400
axeandthrow.com

Smashin' Good Time
1251 Baring Blvd., Sparks, 775-507-4222
smashinrenosparks.com

Truckee River

CULTURE AND HISTORY

PACK COPIOUS CAR SNACKS

AND TAKE A RENO-BASED ROADIE

There's just something about hitting the open road in Nevada: you'll see every kind of terrain imaginable, epic cloud formations, glorious stretches of road that look ominously endless, sagebrush, wild burros, pines, water, and everything in between.

Our friends at Travel Nevada have curated 10 remarkable road-trip experiences throughout Nevada—many of which start or end right here in Northern Nevada. Here are just two with highlights:

Burner Byway: Trace the art-lined route Burners take on their annual pilgrimage "home" to Burning Man. You'll travel from artsy Reno to surreal, tribal-owned Pyramid Lake, to the funky town of Gerlach, and off into the magnificent Black Rock Desert Wilderness.

Cowboy Corridor: This road trip from Reno to West Wendover highlights the confluence of buckaroo, Basque, and American Indian traditions that have shaped the Silver State.

Request a quarterly *Nevada Magazine & Visitor Guide* to help plan your trip, and also download a Highway 50 Survival Guide—a passport you'll stamp along the Loneliest Road in America—at travelnevada.com/travel-guides.

travelnevada.com/road-trips

BEFORE YOU GO, WATCH *WILD NEVADA*

Meet your personal Nevada road trip tour guides: Dave Santina and Chris Orr are hosts of *Wild Nevada*, a travel-destination series on PBS Reno that explores the Silver State.

Each program is filmed over two days, following the pair as they investigate points of interest and reveal insights about Nevada's storied cultural heritage. Explore spots with them like these (and more!):

- Tahoe Rim Trail
- Washoe Lake State Park
- The ominously named Massacre Rim—home to some of the darkest skies in the country

Find your road-trip inspiration by streaming episodes of *Wild Nevada*.

pbsreno.org/watch/wildnevada

65

EAT YOUR ART OUT
AT THE NEVADA MUSEUM OF ART

What you'll likely first notice about the Nevada Museum of Art (NMA) is the drama inherent to the building's exterior. Locals celebrate it as the most resolute work of art at the museum: the black façade, made of creased and folded zinc, is intended to emulate the rock textures found in the nearby Black Rock Desert.

Once inside, you'll be exposed to diverse exhibitions throughout four floors and 70,000 square feet of space. It's an ever-evolving canvas too, as the NMA is undergoing a 50,000-square-foot, $60 million expansion with additional space devoted to permanent collections and an expansion of its Center for Art + Environment.

The NMA is the only art museum in Nevada accredited by the American Alliance of Museums (just 5 percent of all museums in the United States earn this accreditation). Don't miss a visit to the spectacular gift shop, and check the website for the hours of its Café. First feed your literal cravings, then satisfy your more transcendent hunger for exquisite art through time spent perusing the NMA.

160 W Liberty St., 775-329-3333
nevadaart.org

LEARN THE ROPES
AT THE RENO RODEO

No book highlighting Reno's culture would be complete without the Reno Rodeo, a must-attend summertime highlight for more than 100 years. Locals and visitors alike celebrate Nevada's cowboy culture during this 10-day June event, which features bull riding, barrel racing, mutton busting, team roping, and so much more.

A highlight is the annual cattle drive, where wranglers steer (see what we did there?) 300 sauntering cows from Doyle, California, through Nevada's wide-open terrain and into Reno, officially kicking off the rodeo upon their arrival. Did you know that up to 60 guests can join the volunteer cowboys on the journey, living the buckaroo life for the five-day drive? You can join the waitlist from the Reno Rodeo's website.

If you're visiting Reno during non-rodeo time, you can wrangle gear for ranching, roping, and riding at D Bar M Western Store, where the slogan is "Where the cowboys shop." Pretty sure that means you become an honorary cowboy just by shopping there.

D Bar M
1020 E 4th St., 775-329-9107
dbarm.com

Reno Rodeo
775-329-3877
renorodeo.com

67

TAKE A PAGE FROM HISTORY
IN THE DOWNTOWN RENO LIBRARY

For many locals, their childhood weekends were spent scampering among the many floors and sprawling stacks of the Downtown Reno Library, which has seemingly stood frozen in time since its opening. The building, constructed in 1966, still maintains a retro vibe that, when combined with the smell of old books and newsprint, brings some Renoites right back to those early, simpler days.

This branch of the library system still stands as an iconic literary hub, and its architecture and design are a thing to behold. According to library lore, architect Hewitt Wells wasn't allowed to place the library in a park as he'd hoped, so the library's interior was loaned a park-like feel. Hundreds of lush green plants, several full-grown trees, and a pond with a fountain all occupy the building's interior.

301 S Center St., 775-327-8300
washoecountylibrary.us/libraries/downtown-reno.php

GO WHOLE HOG
AT ANDELIN FAMILY FARM

If you're craving a touch of small-town charm while visiting the Biggest Little City, a visit to Andelin Family Farm may be in order. This family-owned farm in Spanish Springs allows you to get up close and personal with a variety of adorable chicks, ducklings, bunnies, piglets, lambs, and calves during the Baby Animal and Tulip Festival, usually spanning a few weekends in the springtime. Admission gives you access to a U-pick field of fresh tulips, as well as a host of barnyard games and activities, including a zipline. The farm also hosts a summer festival with pick-your-own sunflowers, hayrides, and farm animal meet-and-greets.

Of course, the Fall Festival features an expansive pumpkin patch, corn maze, and farm games. For older kids, the popular Corn Creepers Haunted Attraction and Zombie Paintball are destinations for groups of raucous teens looking to enjoy some seriously spooky fun.

Farmer Cameron and his hardworking family are local celebrities to be sure, so stop by, say "hi" to a new friend, and shop for farm-fresh products at Andelin Family Farm.

8100 Pyramid Way, Sparks, 775-530-8032
andelinfamilyfarm.com

69

GET LEGIT GHOSTED
AT THE GOLD HILL HOTEL

Paranormal investigators love Northern Nevada, and for good reason: the boom-and-bust nature of our Comstock Lode history may have left some souls a bit . . . well, stuck. And whether you're a believer or not, we have fun ways to creep into the past with the Silver State's storied specters.

First stop is Virginia City. Make the Silver Queen Hotel, Washoe Club and Haunted Museum, and Mackay Mansion all part of the ghost-hunting itinerary. But don't stop there, as the historic nature of the town makes it rife with (allegedly) supernatural sites.

Just one mile south of Virginia City is the Gold Hill Hotel, established in 1861 and Nevada's oldest operating hotel. The hotel still has original rooms and more contemporary digs, but if you're super brave, ask for the Miner's cabin—which sits under the headframe of the Yellow Jacket Mine. This is the site of the state's worst mining tragedy, where at least 35 miners died in 1869. And rumor has it, they never left.

Visit Virginia City
775-847-7500
visitvirginiacitynv.com

Gold Hill Hotel
1540 Main St., 775-847-0111
goldhillhotel.net

TAKE A SPIRITED WALK

Just down the hill from Virginia City and Gold Hill, Carson City is another fascinating destination full of good old-fashioned ghost stories. And if you're lucky enough to be here between June and October, take the Carson City Ghost Walk, a family-friendly guided tour of history with some "theatrically enhanced" stops along the way.

The tour is led by Madame Curry and the Spirit Wranglers, who tell spooky stories as you explore the Victorian neighborhoods of a bygone era.

Carson City Ghost Walk
775-348-6279
carsoncityghostwalk.com

70

CLIMB THE CLOUDS
AT THE DISCOVERY MUSEUM

Where can you walk on clouds, move a ball using only your brain waves, remove internal organs from a human body without concern, and paint like Leonardo da Vinci? There's only one place that we know of: the Terry Lee Wells Nevada Discovery Museum, known to locals as the Discovery. Visitors ranging in age from 1 to 100 (and beyond!) will soak up this Discovery, a world-class, hands-on science center that sits at the intersection of culture and education, offering exhibits and activities to keep minds thriving.

This is likely not the "typical" museum experience of your early education; in fact, you'll climb, touch, explore, stretch, and grow your brain with fascinating facts—many about Nevada, the American West, and the human body.

The calendar is full of events for children, teens, educators, and parents, including "open build" workshops and guided art lessons. Trust us, this Discovery is monumental!

490 S Center St., 775-786-1000
nvdm.org

71

GET A MARS DELIVERY
IN THE UNR KNOWLEDGE CENTER

While it's not directly from space, the MARS experience on campus at the University of Nevada, Reno, does feel otherworldly. The Mathewson Automated Retrieval System—MARS—is just one of the high-tech highlights of the Mathewson-IGT Knowledge Center, one of the most technologically advanced libraries in the country. This behind-the-scenes, three-story contraption uses six robotic units to get requested materials for patrons.

While you can't specifically visit MARS on campus (it's simply cool to know it's there, doing the hard work), you can explore other parts of the Knowledge Center, head up to the Joe (the university's student union) for a bite to eat, then explore the campus of the state's oldest college. A few "to-do" suggestions:

- Schedule a walking tour of campus.
- Explore Nevada's natural heritage on a self-guided tour of the Museum of Natural History.
- Stop by Morrill Hall, which was built in 1885 and still graces the southern part of campus.
- Walk the elm-lined historic quad.

However you choose to visit, come be a student of higher ed for a day while exploring the remarkable Nevada campus.

University of Nevada, Reno, 1664 N Virginia St., 775-784-1110
unr.edu

72

CALL "ALL ABOARD"
ON THE V&T RAILWAY

During the Comstock Lode, when gold and silver were abundant in the surrounding hills, trains along the V&T—or Virginia and Truckee—used to traverse back and forth from mountains to valleys, transporting the wealth. That's why it's called "Queen of the Shortlines"—its route wasn't long, but the haul was intense.

Today, you can still travel back in time to the bonanza days on the V&T Railway. Authentic steam engines will take you on scenic rides between Carson City and Virginia City or between Virginia City and Gold Hill, or you can explore the Carson River Canyon.

The rides are scheduled seasonally, with some holiday specials—including the popular Polar Express™ during the holiday season. It doesn't get much better than an old steam engine, hot cocoa, and Santa. For an authentic Old West experience, there's perhaps no better ride than the V&T.

4650 Eastgate Siding Rd., Carson City, 833-RAILSNV or 775-686-9037
vtrailway.com

73

EXPLORE RENO'S OVERARCHING SLOGAN

WITH A TRIP DOWNTOWN

Think "Reno," and you'll likely conjure images of the iconic arch and the town's slogan: "Biggest Little City in the World." And the fact is, the arch and the slogan are co-stars in a historic tale of community pride.

The first arch was built in 1926, with the slogan added after a public contest in 1929. Over the decades, Reno has grappled with the question: is the slogan relevant or outdated? But locals now almost universally embrace it and its meaning, quickly pointing out that Reno truly has a classic, small-town vibe with big-city amenities. It serves as a physical reminder that Reno offers the best of both worlds.

And speaking of both worlds: Both an original arch and a modern one grace our downtown—the historic version over Center Street near the National Automobile Museum, and the modern version over Virginia Street in the heart of downtown.

OPEN YOUR "ART" TO THE POSSIBILITIES

AT COPPER CAT STUDIO

Reno's artistic renaissance is in full swing, and makers of every stripe are honing their craft and teaching their mad creative skills to willing students. Interested in painting with watercolor, acrylic, or using the Dutch pour method? We've got classes. Want to take up glassblowing, silversmithing, or jewelry making? You're covered here. Looking to learn about embroidery, crochetwork, or needlepoint? We have "sew" many options.

The region is teeming with artisan spaces where you can learn in a workshop, join a meetup group to socialize and share tips, or shop the creations of gifted artists. Below are just a few highly recommended options:

Atelier
2135 Dickerson Rd., 920-474-6853
atelierinreno.com

Sierra Arts Foundation
17 S Virginia St., 775-329-2787
sierraarts.org

Copper Cat Studio
300 Kresge Ln., Sparks, 775-453-0753
coppercatstudio.com

The Generator
2450 Oddie Blvd., Sparks, 775-527-0633
therenogenerator.com

SHOP TO YOUR ART'S CONTENT AT NEVADA FINE ARTS

Tucked in a corner of a small strip mall in Reno's Midtown is an artisan's version of retail utopia: Nevada Fine Arts has the art supplies you need, abundant workshop space, a lower-level gallery, and creative inspiration for your next project—and it's independently owned!

This art, printing, and framing store also boasts a selection of unique gifts for art aficionados. Visit their website for affordable classes and workshops.

Nevada Fine Arts
1301 S Virginia St., 775-786-1128
nvfinearts.com

SET THE STAGE FOR HISTORIC FUN
AT PIPER'S OPERA HOUSE

What do Mark Twain, Errol Flynn, Al Jolson, President Ulysses S. Grant, and Hal Holbrook all have in common? They've all graced the stage of Piper's Opera House in historic Virginia City.

While not a theatrical venue with a widespread modern reputation, it has a long-storied pedigree as a significant theater attracting national and international stars. From the 1860s until the 1920s, the theater's spotlight fell on some of the most famous faces of stage and screen.

Today, Piper's Opera House is a fully functioning and sought-after performing arts center, with theatrical performances, concerts, and nonprofit events that continue to keep this historic house alive. The opera house is also a working museum with seasonal public tours (April through October) supporting its daily operations.

Also worthy of note is the Old Corner Bar, located on the ground-floor level in the front corner of the building, which is open year-round and attracts its fair share of colorful Virginia City characters.

12 N B St., Virginia City, 775-847-0433
pipersoperahouse.com

76

VISIT NEVADA'S CROWNING GLORY:
OUR STATE CAPITOL

In the centermost portion of Carson City stands a statuesque building with a glistening silver dome. All who travel through the town regard it as the ultimate Nevada symbol: our State Capitol.

In 1870, six years after Nevada entered the union, the structure was constructed in a large lot in the center of a sparsely populated town—the region's forefathers accurately predicting the future growth that would occur. Amazingly, the design for the Nevada State Capitol only cost $250.

History resonates throughout the building, and the public is invited to conduct self-guided tours during operating hours. It's the second-oldest capitol building west of the Mississippi River, and every Nevada governor except the first has had his office in the capitol.

As you explore the grounds, make sure you visit Battle Born Hall—a museum located on the second floor of the Nevada State Capitol building.

101 N Carson St., Carson City
nv.gov or visitcarsoncity.com/attractions/nevada-capitol-building

77

HEADS UP:
IT'S THE WILBUR D. MAY MUSEUM AND ARBORETUM

Anyone from Reno who has ever been on a local museum field trip as a child can tell you exactly how old they were and how they felt the first time they saw the shrunken head. Yup, still traumatized (*raises hand sheepishly*).

But the Wilbur D. May Museum has much more than just a creepy shrunken head and abundant taxidermy (though that's what we likely recall most). The museum is all about the legacy of mid-20th-century Reno businessman/philanthropist Wilbur D. May. The permanent collection highlights exotic artifacts from his 40 trips around the world, his business, and his life.

Outside, the adjacent, far-less-traumatizing arboretum comprises 23 acres, 13 of which serve as a living plant museum with more than 4,000 native and adaptive plant species on display. This is a truly unforgettable museum experience highlighting an important pillar of the community.

But seriously, the eyelashes on that shrunken head . . .

1595 N Sierra St. (inside Rancho San Rafael Regional Park), 775-785-5961
washoecounty.gov/parks/maycenterhome/index.php

Reno's Double Diamond, a residential neighborhood in south Reno, is named after the land that Wilbur May owned in that part of town. His ranch name was a nod to the physical representation of stacking his initials—W and M. Can you see it? Two diamonds, hence Double Diamond Ranch.

78

FEEL THE NEED FOR SPEED
AT THE NATIONAL AUTOMOBILE MUSEUM

Maybe you're a gearhead, maybe you're not—it truly doesn't matter at the National Automobile Museum, as there's something to pique everyone's interest in this massive space.

This museum puts you in the literal driver's seat as you explore about 225 historic cars built from 1892 forward among authentic vintage street scenes and sounds. The majority of the museum's cars are from the world-famous collection of the late Bill Harrah, patriarch of the Harrah family and namesake of the casino hotel chain that got its start just around the corner in downtown Reno.

To add to the fun, you can dress up and sit in a themed photo car for that Instagram snap or visit the museum store for unique gifts and merchandise. Here's an insider scoop: the National Automobile Museum has a podcast studio and a movie theater where it regularly shows films about car and museum history.

Driven to visit yet?

1 Museum Dr., 775-333-9300
automuseum.org

TIP

While at the National Automobile Museum, explore the venue's latest addition—a new outdoor patio with 16,000 square feet of space overlooking the Truckee River. The idyllic setting features fire pits and access to an outdoor bar and can be used for private events or meetings.

79

FOLLOW THE FOOTSTEPS
OF THE DOOMED DONNER PARTY

It's rare that a destination allows you to camp, fish, hike, boat, and stargaze—while at the same time learning about one of the most significantly disastrous human pioneer stories in the history of the West. But that's exactly what happens at Donner Lake, which is a short 45-minute drive from Reno.

Visitors go for Donner Lake's outdoor recreational offerings—which are diverse and abundant year-round—but many are captivated by the true cultural and educational experience at the memorial and visitors center. There you can explore the history of the area and the people who came into this part of the Sierra, including local Native Americans, the Donner Party, and builders of the transcontinental railroad.

Donner Memorial State Park
12593 Donner Pass Rd. at Hwy. 80, Truckee, 530-582-7894
parks.ca.gov/?page_id=503

TIP

On-site at the state park, you'll also find the Pioneer Monument, which was built in the early 1900s. While admiring it, consider this: the stone pedestal is 22 feet high, the same depth as the snow that imprisoned the ill-fated Donner Party for four months. Out of the more than 80 emigrants who embarked on the wagon train, only about half were rescued the following spring. Survivors provided accounts of starvation and of some members of the group resorting to cannibalism.

80

BROWSE RELICS IN MINT CONDITION

AT THE NEVADA STATE MUSEUM

What good is a region built on silver without its own mint, right? City leadership came to that very conclusion back in 1870, establishing the Carson City Mint in our state capital.

Your first steps inside the Nevada State Museum lead you through the former Carson City Mint building, where coins were minted from 1870 to 1893—57 issues of silver, all bearing the distinguishing “CC” mint mark. But the destination is more than solely a historical look at silver; it also houses Native American art and first-person accounts of their experiences in the region. You’ll also see a reconstruction of a Great Basin cave containing evidence of past cultures and climate.

The Nevada State Museum has been open and celebrating the state’s natural and cultural history since October 31, 1941 (which native Nevadans will recognize as Nevada Day, though out-of-staters commonly mistake it as Halloween). It also showcases the importance of Native American, Basque, Chinese, and Latino immigrants and their influence on community and culture.

600 N Carson St., Carson City, 775-687-4810
carsonnvmuseum.org

CHANNEL YOUR INNER BOB ROSS

AT PICASSO & WINE

If you've ever thought to yourself, "Maybe a tree lives right there" while attempting some DIY art, Picasso & Wine is the place for you. And better yet: a glass of wine or a tasty cocktail may just help you decide where your happy trees live.

At Picasso & Wine, Reno's first paint-and-sip, you'll walk in to find a canvas ready to be transformed. After ordering a cocktail (or two—heck, you'll be there for a few hours), you'll get step-by-step instructions from spunky yet capable artists. Remember: no mistakes, just happy accidents.

Best of all, you'll go home with your painting in hand and a newfound appreciation for art. And the end result? Well, you can either donate it to charity, proudly display it on your personal wall of fame/shame, or gift it at your next White Elephant exchange.

Look at you, being all ahead of the gift-giving game.

148 Vassar St., 775-453-1168
picasso-wine.com

BASK IN THE GLOW
OF THE NEON LINE DISTRICT

Sometimes, the best art is the stumble-upon kind. Northern Nevada has a ton of art pieces throughout neighborhoods—many of them having made the journey from the Burning Man playa to their new homes in the heart of Reno.

One notable example is the Neon Line District, which is a concentrated collection of world-class sculptures from Burning Man and beyond. It's situated alongside the J Resort and the Glow Plaza, a festival destination on West 4th Street.

You can also go for one of the area's art walks:

- Explore countless murals and public art pieces in Reno's Midtown. In total, the City of Reno displays 185 pieces of outdoor public art and 65 pieces in the City Hall permanent collection, most notably the Believe statue in City Plaza.
- Take a self-guided walking tour of a curated collection of public art pieces along the Sparks Art Walk. Scanning QR codes along the trail will provide artist statements and details about the pieces.

Neon Line District
renosneonlinedistrict.org

City of Reno Arts & Culture
renoculture.com

Sparks Art Walk
sparksartwalk.com

VISIT A "HOME" FOR ART

The Lake Mansion is the original 1879 home owned by Reno's founder, Myron Lake. But its setting—on the corner of Arlington and Court in downtown Reno—is not its original location. The massive Italianate-style home has traveled not once, but twice through Reno's streets to new locations, making it perhaps the oldest mobile home in Nevada's history.

Arts for All Nevada, a nonprofit offering quality arts programming for all abilities and ages, owns the building and offers workshops and tours.

Arts for All Nevada
250 Court St., 775-826-6100
artsforallnevada.org

Shopping in Virginia City
Photo courtesy of Visit Virginia City, visitvirginiacitynv.com

SHOPPING AND FASHION

83

REDEFINE "VILLAGE PEOPLE"
WHILE SHOPPING RANCHARRAH

The Village at Rancharrah is aptly named, considering the destination is like a self-sustaining town where you can shop to your heart's content, dine on the very best food, take care of your most pressing wellness needs, play, and relax. Really, the only thing missing is your bed. You could easily find a new wardrobe, so don't worry about your absent closet.

This destination for boutique shopping, gourmet dining, and holistic wellness has it all. Parking is close by and abundant, providing convenient access to this walkable outdoor center—home to more than 20 specially curated boutiques, restaurants, bars, and wellness spaces.

Need to relax after all that browsing? No worries. The Village boasts outdoor common areas including a courtyard with a giant chess board, bocce ball court, fireplace, and several seating areas.

Village people? Yup, you're totally one of them now. And you don't even need to don a crazy costume and spell YMCA. Instead, you'll be hitting all the right retail notes at this new village of awesomeness.

7100 Rancharrah Pkwy.
villageatrancharrah.com

HERE ARE JUST A FEW OF THE BOUTIQUES, RESTAURANTS, AND WELLNESS OFFERINGS YOU'LL FIND AT THE VILLAGE AT RANCHARRAH

Bone-ito
Premium pet products for dapper dogs and cool cats.
775-622-8612

Boxwood Avenue
Unique home decor for a simple and fulfilled life.
775-622-3852

Chez Vous
Boutique shopping for home, body, baby, and spirit.
775-826-4948

Dolce Vita
A holistic spa promoting relaxation, wellness, and healthy living.
775-772-0032

Grafted Whiskey and Wine Bar
A spot for carefully crafted share plates and fine drinks.
775-507-2400

84

SAY YES TO THE DRESS (AND EVERYTHING ELSE)
AT LABEL'S

There's a special kind of magic happening at Label's Consignment Boutique, a designer resale shop located in a mid-century retro-vibe building just off the downtown corridor. Somehow, the sales associates seem to instinctively know exactly what will look good on your specific frame and which Hermès scarf would make the perfect accessory. Incredibly, they also know exactly the right size of Christian Louboutins you'll need. And, somehow, they always have a pair.

But the mind reading doesn't end there, as you might also be greeted once you walk in by a very kind associate asking, "Care for a mimosa?" (Hint: the answer to that is always an emphatic "Yes, please!")

All of this is to say, if you're looking for a high-end retail experience with brand-name labels sans the high-end retail brand name price, get thee to Label's. You won't be disappointed. Except . . . you'll be super disappointed when your mimosa is gone. But rumor has it, they have more.

601 W 1st St., 775-825-6000
labelsreno.com

85

READ ALL THE FINE PRINT
AT SUNDANCE BOOKS AND MUSIC

You've likely heard rumor that neighborhood bookstores are remnants of a bygone era—but not true in Reno. We have a thriving independent bookstore scene spearheaded by three totally different literary experiences.

First up is Sundance Bookstore, which resides in the 1906-constructed Levy House and is listed in the US Register of Historic Places. The visual grandeur is only matched by the selection, with gifts, greeting cards, journals—and of course, a delightful selection of books and music.

Speaking of delight, saunter over to The Radical Cat for a purrfectly inspirational experience. It's a feminist bookstore, cat adoption center, and community space all in one. We're not kitten around! (Sorry, it had to be done . . .)

And finally, Grassroots Books is a local gem featuring 40,000-plus books with a constantly changing inventory of used and new selections. You'll find new books and bestsellers at deep discounts, there are huge sales every month, and they even have free book days.

Sundance Books and Music
121 California Ave., 775-786-1188
sundancebookstore.com

Grassroots Books
660 E Grove St., 775-828-2665
grassrootsbooks.com

The Radical Cat
1717 S Wells Ave., 775-409-3152
theradicalcat.square.site

86

CENTER IN
ON RENO'S MIDTOWN DISTRICT

When we're talking unique retail destinations in Reno, 9 out of 10 locals agree: Midtown is the place to be! (And that 10th person doesn't like cool stuff, so they don't matter.)

Here are some highlights of this eclectic neighborhood:

- Midtown is home to more than 150 businesses.
- The area includes 20-plus local restaurants and bars with cuisine from cultures around the world.
- You'll find more than 40 boutiques and shops in Midtown, featuring music, art, fashion, vintage clothing, and more.
- Midtown also boasts 30-plus beauty, wellness, and aesthetic destinations, including tattoo shops, massage and wellness centers, gyms, and salons.
- Keep your eyes open, as more than 50 murals and other artistic and historical installations can be found in Midtown.

Here's our best advice: stroll Midtown's accessible sidewalks. Start on Virginia somewhere to the south of the downtown core, and then just explore the various open doors you'll find along the way.

Visit renomidtown.com for all the deets. In the meantime, the next page has a few recommendations to get you started.

Micano Home

This eclectic space showcases handmade home decor, unique furniture, lighting, and garden art. Artist/owner Sam Sprague creates and curates locally sourced materials to bring you truly unusual conversation starters for your home or modern office.
1350 S Virginia St., 775-329-6422
micanohome.com

Sierra Belle

Fierce, urban, chic, affordable, and practical fashion finds, all wrapped up in an intimate, support-your-fellow-female kinda vibe.
The Sticks Shopping Center, 726 S Virginia St., 775-470-8390
shopsierrabelle.com

Somewhere in Time Antique Mall

Like any good antique mall experience, you never know what you'll find at this collection of antique sellers. Among the specialties: Victorian, rustic farmhouse, railroad memorabilia, mid-century modern, vintage signs, creepy dolls, and more!
1313 S Virginia St., 775-323-1515
somewhereintimereno.com

87

ENJOY A PEAK RETAIL EXPERIENCE
AT THE SUMMIT

Visitors to this upscale, outdoor lifestyle center routinely comment on the year-round, overflowing flowerpots that always seem meticulously maintained. This detail may seem insignificant, but it's the details that set the Summit apart from a typical mall experience.

This is the largest concentration in town of tried, true, and trusted retail names: Dillard's, Apple Store, lululemon athletica, Pottery Barn, MAC, Old Navy, and more. Plus, it's anchored by Century Theatres, meaning you can get your shop on before indulging in popcorn, soft drinks, and the latest Hollywood blockbuster.

The center's modern design offers beautiful pathways connecting stores with nature—sculptures and manicured landscape make browsers feel right at home. Holiday events, fashion shows, and summer farmers markets further connect the community to the Summit experience.

13925 S Virginia St., 775-853-7800
thesummitreno.com

88

PREPARE FOR A SPA-INSPIRING TIME

AT PEPPERMILL AND ATLANTIS

You're in the mood for some pampering—a full day devoted to you. Sounds sublime, right? Well luckily, these two resorts offer the perfect prescription for daylong rejuvenation:

- Peppermill Resort Spa Casino's Spa Toscana comprises three stories (yup, three) and 33,000 square feet of spa space, all bathed in Mediterranean beauty. There, you'll relax in a caldarium that includes an indoor pool, sundeck, and secret garden. Twenty-four treatment rooms offer healthful and revolutionary spa treatments.
- Spa Atlantis features 30,000 square feet of space and amenities such as 16 opulent treatment rooms, a brine inhalation light-therapy lounge, an indoor atrium pool along with an outdoor pool, sundeck, and jetted whirlpool. Known for its exquisite treatments and couples' suites with soaking tubs, steam showers, and a ceremonial chamber, this spa also has unique options to restore body, mind, and spirit.

Spa Toscana
(Peppermill Resort Spa Casino)
2707 S Virginia St., 775-689-7190
spatoscana.com

Spa Atlantis
3800 S Virginia St., 775-954-4135
atlantiscasino.com/spa

RE-BOOT YOUR ADVENTURE GEAR
AT BOBOS

With Reno sitting at the epicenter of adventure paradise, we have many local shops designed for updating your wardrobe, finding the latest gear, and getting tips from experts. Here are two highlights:

- BlueZone Sports is a regional family of outdoor gear stores encircling Lake Tahoe. This makes it an ideal spot for snow and water equipment, bike gear, and clothing and accessories for hiking, camping, backpacking, and outdoor adventure. A "blue zone" refers to places in the world where people live longer—we can't guarantee a longer life shopping here, but you'll certainly be living your best life accompanied by the right gear for your next Sierra excursion!
- BOBOS was founded by the legendary local Sheehan family—former Olympic ski coach Robert "Bobo" was the patriarch, and daughter Patty would eventually become a golf Hall of Famer. Owing to their family passions and epic skills, they opened this tried-and-true destination for ski equipment in 1969. It now boasts a huge selection of gear for all winter sports, as well as patio and outdoor furniture.

BlueZone Sports
Multiple locations, 844-786-6486
bluezonesports.com

BOBOS
475 E Moana Ln., 775-826-9096
bobos.com

WALK THE PLANKS
IN VIRGINIA CITY

As you shuffle along the authentic wood-planked paths of Virginia City, admiring the detailed and historic façades of the surrounding buildings, you'll be surprised by the variety of retail options you encounter. Vintage-inspired shops with native jewelry and mercantiles with Old West souvenirs and Western-style clothing are the norm, obviously. But so are beautiful antiques, as well as places to pose for old-time photos—the latter being a favorite among children who want to play dress up.

Don't miss Grandma's Fudge Factory, a Virginia City institution since 1971. And make sure to stop into local restaurants and saloons—especially if there's a live musician playing, as you might just discover your next favorite local artist. Also be on the lookout for museums, mines, and cemeteries—some of them promising a potential spook or two.

Visit Virginia City
86 S C St., Virginia City, 775-847-7500
visitvirginiacitynv.com

91

GET A BIRD'S-EYE VIEW
OF RETRO RICHES AT THE NEST

Je ne sais quoi literally means "I don't know what" in French. And that can't-quite-put-your-finger-on-it vibe is exactly what these destinations have—an indescribable flair that makes them top of the list for locals looking for that perfect new-old treasure.

At The Nest, owner Tessa Dee Miller has created a refuge for beautiful vintage heirlooms, clothing, furniture, and accessories. Better still, she has an eye for art and creates chic, sometimes playful vignettes that inspire your creativity. Stop by often for her ever-changing inventory. Be prepared for a fabulous customer service experience that makes you feel truly seen.

Junkee Clothing Exchange is known as THE destination for costumes and playa wear. Shoppers often go in with specific ideas in mind—the need for a retro-inspired dress, a specific cosplay piece, or an accessory request—and the Junkee team helps find—or create—the solution. You also can find antiques, furniture, and records by exploring their "sister" store, Uncle Junkee.

The Nest
201 Keystone Ave., 775-284-8841
thenestreno.com

Junkee Clothing Exchange
Reno Public Market, 299 E Plumb Ln.
Uncle Junkee, 111 N Virginia St., 775-322-5865
junkeeclothingexchange.com

92

FIND FUN FOR EVERYONE
AT OUTLETS AT LEGENDS

While we don't often associate retail therapy with the idea of expanding our brains, that's exactly the delicate balance struck at the Outlets at Legends. The open-air retail and entertainment destination is perfect for history buffs and art aficionados who also enjoy shopping, considering sculptures paying homage to Nevada legends such as Dat-So-La-Lee, Mark Twain, and the region's Pony Express riders dot the landscape.

The Outlets at Legends is also a great place for kids and their parents—especially during warmer months, when fountains entertain children (bring a suit and a towel) and parents can overlook the fun from adjacent benches (or splash around too!).

Of course, there's shopping and entertainment: many of the locations are outlets, offering deep discounts to savvy shoppers. There's Scheels serving as an anchor—with its indoor Ferris wheel, invented by Nevadan George W. Ferris, a must-ride highlight—and Galaxy IMAX theater as another. Just recently, the region's first new casino in 20 years, Legends Bay Casino, opened its doors to eager guests.

1310 Scheels Dr., Sparks, 775-358-3800
reddevelopment.com/outlets-at-legends

93

BREATHE IN THE FLOWER POWER
AT MOANA NURSERY

In search of a gift or treasure direct from Mother Nature? Here are a few fragrant options:

- Browse Moana Nursery's expansive nurseries and garden centers to discover a wide selection of flowers, unique gifts, and quirky stuff for the garden. If you're looking for a gift for the green thumb in your life (or maybe it's you?), this favorite local shop has stunning indoor plants in its greenhouse; pottery, garden, and patio accessories; gifts; fountains; and statuary.
- You know what's better than the smell of flowers? The smell of flowers AND coffee. The Garden of Reno offers an experience that coalesces these two perennial favorites, with a coffee lounge and flower shop sharing the same beautiful building in the up-and-coming Wells Avenue District. Did you ever notice that "bouquet" and "latte" sorta rhyme? How about that?

Moana Nursery
Multiple locations, 775-825-0602
moananursery.com

The Garden of Reno
700 S Wells Ave., 775-440-1019
thegardenofreno.com

When you leave the Garden of Reno—Americano and cream cheese Danish in hand—make sure you spend some time exploring the burgeoning Wells Avenue District. This picturesque and multicultural historic business district totals about 1.5 miles and comprises boutiques, restaurants, and coffee shops. So pick a direction and browse this walkable district!

COOK UP SOME FUN
AT NOTHING TO IT!

Seems like we're all now spending more time in the kitchen, so to satisfy your craving for the coolest gadgets and gourmet goodies, read on.

Nothing To It! Culinary Center is like Disneyland for foodies. The quaint kitchen store has a huge selection of tools, utensils, and thingamabobs. Warning: browsing the selection may convince you to purchase things you didn't even know existed. Forewarned is forearmed!

The store is a gateway to the Nothing To It! Cooking School, which offers classes on a variety of topics (recent options: artisan pizza, dim sum, knife skills).

With new gadgets in hand and skills enhanced, head to Big Horn Olive Oil Company to browse the largest selection of specialty balsamic vinegars and olive oils you've EVER seen. But that's not all: their shelves are a browsing utopia of olives, spices, honey, and gadgets. Ask for input on pairings—I recently left with a cranberry pear balsamic to complement my olive oil purchase.

Nothing To It! Culinary Center
225 Crummer Ln., 775-826-2628
nothingtoit.com

Bighorn Olive Oil Company
3888 Mayberry Dr., (775) 870-1500
bhooc.com

95

GRAB GROCERIES TO GO
FROM LOCAL FARMERS MARKETS

The freshest, healthiest foods don't come from store shelves; they come from local farms. And Northern Nevada has a vibrant farmers market scene that is bringing tasty, earth-friendly offerings to local shoppers.

The Riverside Farmers Market is Reno's only year-round market, happening Saturday mornings from 9 a.m. to noon. From micro-farms and home-based bakers to small business owners and ranchers, they connect local producers with eager shoppers at the McKinley Arts & Culture Center.

Shirley's Farmers Markets produces two local events: The longest-running market in Reno happens Saturday mornings starting at 8 a.m. from June to October at the Village Market on California Avenue, and the Tamarack Junction Farmers Market, which takes place from 9 a.m. to 1 p.m., also happens on Saturdays during the months from late spring to early fall.

Make plans to come browse the booths and score some fresh, fabulous finds during any of these homegrown events.

Riverside Farmers Market
925 Riverside Dr.
renofarmersmarket.com

Shirley's Farmers Markets
The Village, 1119 California Ave.
Tamarack Junction Casino, 13101 S Virginia St.
shirleysfarmersmarkets.com

FUN IS IN STORE—LITERALLY
AT TOYS N MORE

Independent toy stores are a treasure trove, offering unexpected playful finds among aisles of smiles. The customer service experience can't be beat at these local retail gems, so if you have questions about the most popular Squishmallow or fidget spinner, just ask.

Toys N More is a delightful destination for educational toys, throwback games, and stuffies. The spacious location has a separate room full of barrels of saltwater taffy and other sweet treats, making this a one-of-a-kind bulk candy store experience as well.

Learning Express also features toys to educate and inspire creativity such as puzzles, science kits, and costumes. They even have an arts section with pencil cases, lap desks, clipboards, and more that they'll personalize with your child's name at no charge.

Finally, if you're looking for the perfect creative gift for a child (or child at heart), visit Kelekia. It's a magical place full of creative, smile-inducing, innovative toys and games.

Toys N More
4809 Kietzke Ln., Ste. C, 775-384-1044
toysnmoreofreno.com

Kelekia Toys & Gifts
3886 Mayberry Dr., 775-453-2999
kelekiatoys.com

Learning Express
197 Damonte Ranch Pkwy., Ste. D, 775-853-7884
learningexpress.com/reno

CELEBRATE GOOD TIMES AT THIS STORE!

If you're in the market for toys, there's a good chance there's a party in your future. So if you're also looking for a locally owned place to pick up party favors and goodie bag supplies, balloons or decorative centerpieces, or themed merch for upcoming holidays, visit Party America.

The stock in this expansive store is indeed diverse, including liquor (talk about a one-stop shop!) and a huge selection of inexpensive cards. Here's a fun find: they have an array of "Greetings from Reno" type cards, which are super cool to send to out-of-staters. The fact that this is a family-owned party store is icing on the proverbial cake.

Speaking of icing, pretty sure they have that too . . .

Party America Reno
5925 S Virginia St., 775-825-0825
partyamericareno.com

SHOP MODERN HOME—WITH HUMOR

AT WHITE DAISY DESIGNS

Now and then, you walk into a local store that simply feels like home. That's the case with the home-plus-so-much-more stores you'll read about here.

White Daisy Designs in Sparks is a treasure trove of stuff you didn't know you need—but you totally need. First, check if Hank the store dog is there to get your fluffy-friend fix. Then it's off to browse gifts for animal lovers, signs with quirky messages, Nevada-themed treasures, clothing, candles, and so much more. (TIP: If you're tired of buying a new welcome sign for every season, they have handmade signs with seasonal magnetic interchangeable pieces. So smart!)

Across town in Reno, Red Chair invites you to browse mid-century, modern, and Danish furnishings and accessories among a 5,600-square-foot showroom. Or perhaps you're interested in a more vintage take on home shopping? The Vassar House is a fun and funky destination, with uniquely curated home-décor and gift options.

White Daisy Designs
171 Los Altos Pkwy., Sparks
775-376-1975
facebook.com/whitedaisyreno

The Vassar House
221 Vassar St.
775-825-2180
luckystargallery.com

Red Chair
3400 Lakeside Dr., 775-770-0111

FEED BODY, SOUL, AND SPIRIT AT SOUTH CREEK

Have a few hours to discover your new favorite local haunt? Head to the corner of South Virginia and South Meadows Parkway to visit South Creek, a shopping center and entertainment plaza where the many doorways lead to fun, food, and finds!

Go for the shopping—stay for the food. That's the first tip to tackling the South Creek experience. You'll find locally owned boutiques and jewelry shops and even a place to pamper your pooch. A sampling of favorites includes G. J. Rhodes Gift & Home, BVW Jewelers, and Healthy Tails. All that shopping will work up an appetite, so stop by Yosh's Unique Deli for a scrumptious sandwich, Bibo for a chai latte, or Batch Cupcakery for a sweet treat.

Then, there's the soul-infusion portion of your visit. For the grownups, there are unique and pampering destinations such as Icebox Cryotherapy, The Center Foundation for some mindfulness meditation, or Soak for a mani-pedi. For the tiny humans, there's even a Tutu School!

95 Foothill Rd.
southcreeknv.com

99

SHOP THE NEVADA LEGISLATIVE GIFT SHOP

FOR SILVER STATE SWAG

If the previous 98 entries don't give you reason enough to be a Nevada convert, we don't know what will! Clearly, now's the time to shop for that commemorative souvenir to show off your Silver State pride.

While there are many places to pick up your Nevada-themed gear, this may be the coolest, experience-wise: the Nevada Legislative Gift Shop, which sits in Room 1189 of the Legislative Building in Carson City (right next door to our gorgeous silver-domed Capitol).

Spend the day touring the Capitol, and then end your journey in this unique store. You'll find merchandise for the kitchen, such as state-shaped cutting boards and coasters. You'll find stuffies for the kids in the shape of animals you'd find roaming Nevada's hills. You'll find books, stickers for your hydration vessel of choice, jewelry with pendants in the shape of Lake Tahoe, ornaments, and so much more.

Better yet, during the legislative season, you might just be shopping alongside one of our state's public servants!

401 S Carson St., Carson City, 775-684-6800
shop.leg.state.nv.us/giftshop

TIP

Try the following spots for stickers, gear, gift baskets, books, clothing, themed merchandise, and everything you can imagine that screams "Silver State"—the options are endless!

Home Means Nevada Co.
Multiple locations
homemeansnevada.com

The Flag Store
155 Glendale Ave., Ste. 9, Sparks, 775-355-0506
eventflags.com

Nevada Gift Shop
1013 S Carson St., Carson City, 775-882-2600

Nevada Marketplace
4001 S Virginia St. in Reno Town Mall, 775-384-3153
buynevadafirst.com

100

SOAK UP THE HEALING VIBES AT STEAMBOAT HOT SPRINGS

You've done it! You've browsed 100 entries, which means you've earned a heaping dose of relaxation. Nevada claims to be home to more naturally occurring hot springs than any state, so here are a few ways to seduce your soul into soaking submission:

Steamboat Hot Springs was named by legendary Nevadan Mark Twain. Witness puffs of steam billowing skyward as you approach, resulting from a rumbling below that Twain compared to "a steamboat in motion." Locals have been soaking in the healing properties of these volcanic waters since 1857, but the current destination offers a therapeutic experience in colorful rooms with stained glass features targeting your chakras.

Carson Hot Springs has also been enticing bathers with the curative properties of thermal spring water since the 1800s. Kids are welcome at this literal hot spot, with an outdoor swimming pool maintained at about 95 degrees in summer and 100 in winter. Indoor private pools are also available.

Steamboat Hot Springs
16010 S Virginia St., 775-853-6600
steamboatsprings.org

Carson Hot Springs
1500 Old Hot Springs Rd., Carson City, 775-885-8844
carsonhotsprings.com

ACTIVITIES
BY SEASON

SPRING

SUMMER

FALL

WINTER

SUGGESTED ITINERARIES

CREATIVE DATE-NIGHT DINING

GET YOUR CULTURE ON

DATES WITH A SIDE OF ADVENTURE

FUN FOR THE HISTORY BUFF

LOOKING TO FEED THE FAMILY?

IF YOU WANT TO GROW YOUR BRAIN

WHEN THE KIDS ARE DRIVING YOU BONKERS

YOU DESERVE A DAY OF PAMPERING

DRINK IN THE ADULTS-ONLY TIME

INDEX